The Authorship of the Pseudo-Dionysian Corpus

This monograph revisits one of the most debated aspects of Dionysian scholarship: the enigma of its authorship. To establish the identity of the author remains impossible. However, the legitimacy of the attribution of the corpus to Dionysius the Areopagite should not be seen as an intended forgery but rather as a masterfully managed literary device, which better indicates the initial intention of the actual author. The affiliation with Dionysius the Areopagite has metaphorical and literary significance. Dionysius is the only character in the New Testament who is unique in his conjunction between the apostle Paul and the Platonic Athenian Academy. In this regard this attribution, to the mind of the actual author of the corpus, could be a symbolic gesture to demonstrate the essential truth of both traditions as derived essentially from the same divine source. The importance of this assumption taken in its historical context highlights the culmination of the formation of the civilized Roman-Byzantine Christian identity.

Vladimir Kharlamov gained his PhD in Theological and Religious Studies at Drew University, US. His research in Pseudo-Dionysius and deification is closely connected with issues of interrelationship and dialogue between the emerging Christian Roman-Byzantine identity and the society of Late Antiquity at large.

The Authorship of the Pseudo-Dionysian Corpus
A Deliberate Forgery or Clever Literary Ploy?

Vladimir Kharlamov

LONDON AND NEW YORK

First published 2020 by Routledge

2 Park Square, Milton Park, Abingdon, Oxon OX14 4RN
605 Third Avenue, New York, NY 10017

Routledge is an imprint of the Taylor & Francis Group, an informa business

First issud in paperback 2021

Copyright © 2020 Vladimir Kharlamov

The right of Vladimir Kharlamov to be identified as author of this work has been asserted by him in accordance with sections 77 and 78 of the Copyright, Designs and Patents Act 1988.

All rights reserved. No part of this book may be reprinted or reproduced or utilised in any form or by any electronic, mechanical, or other means, now known or hereafter invented, including photocopying and recording, or in any information storage or retrieval system, without permission in writing from the publishers.

Notice:

Product or corporate names may be trademarks or registered trademarks, and are used only for identification and explanation without intent to infringe.

Publisher's Note

The publisher has gone to great lengths to ensure the quality of this reprint but points out that some imperfections in the original copies may be apparent.

British Library Cataloguing-in-Publication Data
A catalogue record for this book is available from the British Library

Library of Congress Cataloging-in-Publication Data
A catalog record for this book has been requested

ISBN: 978-0-367-43812-8 (hbk)
ISBN: 978-1-03-217666-6 (pbk)
DOI: 10.4324/9781003005971

Typeset in Times New Roman
by Apex CoVantage, LLC

Contents

Acknowledgements	vi
Abbreviations for editions and collections	vii
Abbreviations for primary works	viii
Introduction	1
1 Attempts to justify pseudonymous affiliation	10
2 Known and conventionally accepted facets of the *CD* in relation to its authorship	20
3 How serious was the author of the *CD* about the first-century environment?	47
4 The Dionysian society	54
5 The metaphorical symbolism of the attribution	68
Conclusion	78
Selected bibliography	85
Index	92

Acknowledgements

I would like to express my gratitude to Matthew Gruchow and Stephen Finlan for their indispensable help with proofreading this book.

Abbreviations for editions and collections

CD *Corpus Dionysiacum*
GCS Die griechischen christlichen Schriftsteller der ersten Jahrhunderte. Berlin: Akademie-Verlag, 1897—.
LCL Loeb Classical Library. Cambridge, MA: Harvard University Press, 1912—.
PG J. P. Migne, ed. Patrologiae cursus completus, Series Graeca. 166 vols. Paris, 1857–1886.
PTS Patristische Texte und Studien. Berlin: Walter de Gruyter, 1964—.
SC H. de Lubac, J. Daniélou, et al., eds. Sources Chrétiennes. Paris: Éditions du Cerf, 1941—.

Abbreviations for primary works

Clement of Alexandria
Strom.   *Stromata*

Eunapius
VS   *Vitae Sophistarum*

Eusebius of Caesarea
EH   *Historia Ecclesiastica*
PE   *Praeparatio Evangelica*

Gregorius of Naziansus
Ep.   *Epistulae*
Or.   *Orationes*

John of Scythopolis
SchCH   *Scholia De caelesti hierarchia*
SchDN   *Scholia De divinis nominibus*
SchEp   *Scholia Epistulae*

John Philoponus
Prol.   *Prologus*

Plato
Symp.   *Symposium*

Proclus
In Parm.   *In Platonis Parmenidem commentarii*
In Tim.   *In Platonis Timaeum commentarii*

Pseudo-Dionysius Areopagita
CH   *De caelesti hierarchia*
EH   *De ecclesiastica hierarchia*
DN   *De divinis nominibus*
MT   *De mystica theologia*
Ep.   *Epistulae*

Introduction

Until the Renaissance the *Areopagitica* was accepted as an orthodox and authentic collection of works authored by Dionysius the Areopagite mentioned in Acts 17:34. Peter Abelard (1079–1142) was one of few lonely voices who attempted to stir some controversy around the corpus, but even such a sharp mind as his did not in principle question the orthodoxy of the *CD*'s content. Abelard simply challenged the false identification of Dionysius of Paris with Dionysius the Areopagite. With coming of the Renaissance, the situation noticeably changed. Lorenzo Valla in 1457, William Grocyn in 1501, and Erasmus in 1504 seriously doubted the identity of the authorship. Many others, especially in Protestant camp, followed suit. Martin Luther, in his peculiar style, categorically dismissed the corpus and asked everybody to stay away "from that Dionysius, whoever he was."[1]

In a more constructive direction, Johann Engelhardt pointed out in 1820 the dependence of the *CD* on Proclus's Neoplatonic philosophy.[2] While Engelhardt failed to provide detailed linkage between Proclus and the *CD*, by the close of the nineteenth century Hugo Koch[3] and Josef Stiglmayr[4] independently confirmed and documented this link and firmly established the pseudonymous character of the *Areopagitica*. Hence, I retain the use of "pseudo" before Dionysius the Areopagite when referring to the author of the *CD*. I do so not as a sign of disrespect or attestation to malicious fraudulence on the part of the actual author, but simply as the evidence of historical accuracy.

Dependence of the *CD* on Proclus (d. 485) sets the *terminus a quo* for the date of this corpus. Venance Grumel, drawing on the Pseudo-Dionysian use of Proclus's *Commentary on the First Alcibiades*, proposes the date for the corpus to be after 462.[5] The first citation of the corpus by the Monophysite bishop Severus of Antioch (d. 538) sets the *terminus ante quem*. To date Severus's own works with precision is difficult. As Paul Rorem and John Lamoreaux point out, "The first firm date, . . . is 528 the year in which Severus' treatises against Julian were translated into Syriac, though the treatises themselves may have been composed as many as nine years earlier—exactly when we know not."[6] They personally consider the possible date for composition of the *CD* close to the date of its first appearance, "for it is hard to imagine that the corpus would have left no mark for decades, or that an author as resourceful as the mysterious Dionysius would not have made sure that his work was 'discovered' sooner rather than later."[7] Rosemary Arthur also argues for a later date for composition of the *CD*, between 527–532, and places the origin of this corpus in Syrian Monophysitism. She, however, believes that quotations of the *CD* in writings of Severus are later editorial additions.[8] Beate Suchla sets 476, the year when Peter the Fuller introduced recital of the Creed to the liturgy,[9] as the earliest possible date and 518/528, when references to the corpus attested in writings of Severus of Antioch, as the latest.[10] The liturgical environment in the *CD* reflects several elements that are close to ones in which Peter the Fuller was involved, which made Peter one of possible proposed candidates for the authorship of the corpus.[11] Use of these works by Severus of Antioch, already as authoritative texts, along with some other internal evidence, immediately suggested the Syrian origin. Stiglmayr was the first to propose fifth-century Syria-Palestine as the place of origin.[12] He later also proposed Severus as a possible author.[13] However, we still know nothing with certainty about who exactly was the first to discover this corpus and where.

After the discoveries of Koch and Stiglmayr any hopes that Dionysius the Areopagite from the first century was the actual author assertively dissipated. Since then, the seemingly endless, often creative and imaginative search for the author's true identity, involving a long list of proposed candidates, did not actually bear any convincing results. At the same time, it never ceased to disturb academic minds. The mystical attraction of the *Areopagitica* commences with the mystery of the author.

The conviction that the *Areopagitica* was *obviously* intended to be perceived as written by Dionysius the Areopagite is still deeply entrenched in modern scholarship. For example, István Perczel insists, "The fiction that the author was Dionysius the Areopagite, the Athenian judge who converted to Christianity upon hearing Paul's famous speech from Acts 17, seems to be the cornerstone of the *CD*."[14] Such a tendency is understandable. After centuries when the *Areopagitica* experienced uncontested widespread influence in great degree due to its association with the name of Dionysius the Areopagite, it is hard to imagine that it could be otherwise.

In modern scholarship this affiliation, with a few notable exceptions discussed in the first chapter, is vehemently interpreted as a malicious forgery—a conscious attempt to deceive and mislead. Hence, the search for the true identity of the author unleashed such frenzy that it became the main emphasis of the Dionysian question, often at the expense of broader contents of the corpus and its intellectual significance.[15] The trouble with identifying the true authorship endures as one of the main foci of Dionysian research.[16]

What Dionysian scholarship often ignores is rather meager evidence in the text of the corpus that might support the intentional desire to present this corpus as coming from the first century. The emphasis on the attribution of these works to the historical Dionysius the Areopagite can also be a later editorial and defensive strategy of supporters, *the first enthusiastic readers*, of this corpus to ease its acceptance in order to promote or legitimize its contents, which otherwise might be quite problematic. The evidence for—or at least the possibility of—editorial interference was suggested on several occasions. They will be appropriately referenced later. Besides, as John Copp correctly observes, " 'Pseudo' was and is common to scholars when dating is unknown or authenticity in question, (e.g., Pseudo-Grosseteste, Pseudo-Hierotheos, Pseudo-Symeon) and is used in a non-judgmental way."[17] In the case of Pseudo-Dionysius, however, many scholars assume viciousness on the part of the author to deceive everybody with his or, perhaps *her*, forgery so that purely Neoplatonic content, in the view of some scholars presented as devoid of anything genuinely Christian, can freely circulate under a Christian name. Even scholars sympathetic to the Christian content of the corpus while dealing with the authorship issue still justify attribution of the corpus to Dionysius the Areopagite as due to some kind of mystical connection of the actual author to the historical Dionysius, rather than acknowledging the rather limited significance of this attribution to the main content of the corpus.

It is important to emphasize that early commentators on the *Areopagitica*, John of Scythopolis and John Philoponus, were not ignorant of the *CD*'s Neoplatonic content and chronological discrepancies that some allegedly historical references to first-century Christianity might present. While mostly avoiding detailed discussion of chronological discrepancies, after briefly acknowledging the Neoplatonic content they attempt to reverse the argument and make Neoplatonic philosophers dependent on the *Areopagitica* rather than the other way around. In the Prologue to the Dionysian corpus in the Migne edition[18] there are two passages that Suchla attributes to John Philoponus.[19] These two passages address problems of origin and Neoplatonism in the *CD*. In one, John Philoponus objects to accusations of forgery. In his opinion, it is impossible for the author of the corpus, "who is capable to go beyond sense perceptions and come into contact with noetic beauty and through this to reach as far as possible God," to be so wicked as to present himself as a contemporary and correspondent of the apostles, a witness of the solar eclipse at the time of Christ's death, and being present at the time of the Dormition of the Mother of God, if these were not true accounts. In another passage, Philoponus writes, "One must know that some of the non-Christian philosophers, especially Proclus have often employed certain concepts of the blessed Dionysius. . . . It is possible to conjecture from this that the ancient philosophers in Athens usurped his works . . . and then hid them, so that they themselves might seem to be the progenitors of his divine oracles."[20] A similar approach, asserting the dependency of Proclus on Pseudo-Dionysius and other Christian sources rather than of Pseudo-Dionysius on Proclus (although not on Dionysius the Areopagite of the first century), was suggested recently by Ilaria Ramelli.[21]

Occasionally, proposed solutions for the identity of the author might be viewed as lying on the borderline of academic research and literary fiction. To some degree the genre of fiction is unavoidable when we deal with a set of documents about which we know almost nothing for certain regarding the circumstances that inspired their writing, their geographical milieu, exact time of their origin, or the person of the author who produced them. Apart from conjecture that the author was either a younger contemporary of Proclus or belonged to the generation that immediately followed him, the didactic nature of the *CD* makes its contextualization extremely problematic. If this corpus were explicitly polemical, it could significantly simplify finding its *Sitz im Leben*.[22] Hence, it is not surprising that for some the author of the *Areopagitica* can be imagined as an aging monastic bishop behind the desk in his cell who writes down the fruits of his life-long study, reflection, and ascetical experience.[23] With similar ease others might see him as a young man who probably was initially non-Christian, but at some point during his studies in either Athens or Alexandria underwent conversion to Christianity and who, instead of denouncing his Neoplatonic learning, composed the most sophisticated and original system of Christian philosophy incorporating Neoplatonic and Patristic insights.[24]

If Caroline Putnam in 1960 had a more optimistic perspective when she suggested that "perhaps another century will unravel the mystery of the 'Pseudo-Denis'"[25] then Alexander Golitzin, in the opening of that next century, arrived at a more realistic conclusion: "We simply do not know who Dionysius was, nor, barring new evidence, will we ever know."[26] In the current state of affairs Paul Rorem correctly observes, "There is . . . no historical basis for an investigation of the spirituality of this author except for his pseudonymous writings, which are so intentionally misleading about their original context and community."[27]

I wish I could claim this book finally solves the mystery of the author's identity. My intentions, however, are different. I do not try to solve the mystery of the author's identity. I propose several suggestions that could throw light on the legitimacy of such attribution not as an intended forgery, but rather as a masterfully managed literary device, a practice that was not that uncommon for Late Antiquity. Iamblichus, for example, published his famous *De Mysteriis*, where he argues with his mentor Porphyry, under the name of the Egyptian prophet Abamon, while his authorship was well attested by Proclus and probably by Porphyry himself. The reason why Iamblichus did it might be that of courtesy to his mentor, perhaps he did not want to appear to argue against Porphyry openly. There is also whole tradition of Hermetic and Pythagorean literature, which was attributed respectively to Hermes and Pythagoras, while their readers were well aware that neither of these authors actually wrote these works; however, they still were considered to be authentic as being authentically inspired by Hermes and Pythagoras.[28] Hans Urs von Balthasar makes a similar argument in defense of Dionysian authenticity.[29] Another good example is *Wisdom of Solomon*, written in Greek at the end of the first century BCE or in the beginning of the first century CE by an anonymous author. It was accepted as an authoritative book not only by Hellenized Jews but also by Church fathers, and later found its place among deuterocanonical books in the Roman Catholic and most of Eastern Orthodox Bibles, even though the pseudepigraphical nature of this work was not a secret for ancient readers.[30] Pseudo-Dionysius, for example, refers to *Wisdom of Solomon* as "the introduction to the Scriptures."[31] As Stephen Gersh, questioning "whether the author of the *CA* intended his pseudonymic writing to be understood by its potential readers as an authentic production or as a literary fiction" observes, "Pseudonymic works were often simply intended to be taken as such follows from widespread practice in the higher schools of antiquity of composing fictitious speeches and letters as though by historical personages as a form of rhetorical training."[32]

Dionysius the Areopagite (Acts 17:16–34) is the only character in the New Testament who is unique in his conjunction between the apostle Paul and Greek philosophy. He is one where "Athens" meets "Jerusalem"—a Christian student of philosophers and of the apostle Paul, a living testimony of apostolicity and the Athenian Academy. In this regard the attribution of the corpus to his pen could be a symbolic gesture to demonstrate the essential truth of both traditions as essentially derived from the same divine source, which to some degree was confirmed by the authority of the apostle Paul in his "Unknown God" sermon.[33] Such a claim, regardless of its theological implications to the taste of some contemporary critics, was not uncommon for Patristic apologetics.[34] For Patristic apologists any truth found in Plato is in its essence Christian truth: "What is Plato, but Moses who speaks Attic Greek?"[35]

This assumption, taken in the historical context when the *CD* was written, points to the culminating stage of the formation of what could be termed the civilized Roman-Byzantine Christian identity. The identity that, to the mind of the ancients, would comply with both the cultural standards of Hellenistic antiquity and the uninterrupted succession of Christian tradition, where any tension between being a true citizen of the Roman Empire and a Christian were disappearing. The initial popularity of the *CD* (modest at the beginning)[36] also, to some degree, could be explained as being the most suitable response to the cultural development of the time.[37]

The first chapter presents a brief assessment of recent attempts to justify pseudonymous affiliation of the corpus with Dionysius the Areopagite of the Book of Acts. In the second chapter, this book proceeds with discussion of authorship topics that are usually presented in Dionysian scholarship as conventionally accepted facts. The actual author's Syrian background, his familiarity with Athenian Neoplatonism, the Christianity of Pseudo-Dionysius, and the integrity of the corpus and its influence are discussed. The third chapter questions the legitimacy of pseudonymous attribution as the deliberate intention of the anonymous author. I do not propose, however, a radical denial that the author of the corpus made some efforts to create this impression. I simply argue that the evidence in the corpus that is seen as suggesting this attribution does not present a strong and overwhelming case, especially in establishing historical contextualization of the first century. I argue that it was not the main intention of the actual author to present his work as an authentic first-century production. Assigning Dionysius the Areopagite as the author of the corpus has literary significance, rather than attempting to project historical affiliation. The fourth chapter that deals with the so-called Dionysian society develops this argument further. The fifth chapter sums up the main arguments for symbolic and metaphorical attribution of the corpus to the Areopagite.

Notes

1 Cit. in Alexander Golitzin, "Dionysius Areopagita: A Christian Mysticism?" *Pro Ecclesia* 12 (2003): 161.
2 Johann G. Engelhardt, *Dissertatio de Dionysio Areopagita plotinizante praemissis observationibus de historia theologiae mysticae rite tractanda: Sectio secunda quam auctoritate reverendissimi theologorum ordinis in Academia Friderico-Alexandrina die 28 Nov. MDCCCXX. horis pomeridianis respondente pro facultate docendi publico iudicio submittet* (Erlangae: Typis Hilpertianis, 1820). Cf. Sarah Klitenic Wear and John Dillon, *Dionysius the Areopagite and the Neoplatonist Tradition* (Hampshire, UK: Ashgate, 2007), 3.
3 Hugo Koch, "Proklus als Quelle des Pseudo-Dionysius Areopagita in der Lehre vom Bösen," *Philologus* 54 (1895): 438–54; idem, *Pseudo-Dionysius Areopagita in Seinen Beziehungen zum Neuplatonismus und Mysterienwesen* (Mainz: Verlag von Franz Kirchleim, 1900).
4 Josef Stiglmayr, "Der Neuplatoniker Proclus als Vorlage des sog. Dionysius Areopagita in der Lehre vom Übel," *Historisches Jahrbuch* 16 (1895): 253–73, 721–48, etc.

Introduction 7

5 Venance Grumel, "Autour de la question pseudo-Dionysienne," *Revue des études Byzantines* 13 (1955): 21.
6 Paul Rorem and John C. Lamoreaux, *John of Scythopolis and the Dionysian Corpus: Annotating the Areopagite* (Oxford: Clarendon Press, 1998), 10.
7 Rorem and Lamoreaux, *John of Scythopolis and the Dionysian Corpus*, 11.
8 Rosemary A. Arthur, *Pseudo-Dionysius as Polemicist: The Development and Purpose of the Angelic Hierarchy in Sixth Century Syria* (Burlington, VT: Ashgate, 2008), 104–9.
9 Cf. *EH* 3.3.7, 436CD.
10 Beate Regina Suchla, *Dionysius Areopagita: Leben, Werk, Wirkung* (Wien: Herder, 2008), 21–22.
11 See Michaelis Lequien, "De quibusdam auctoritatibus, quibus Eutychesaliique unius in Christo nature assertores haeresim suam tuebantur," in PG 94:261–314; Utto Riedinger, "Pseudo-Dionysios Areopagites, Pseudo-Kaisarios und die Akoimeten," *Byzantinische Zeitschrift* 52 (1956): 276–96.
12 Stiglmayr, "Das Aufkommen der ps.-dionysischen Schriften und ihr Eindringen in die christliche Literatur bis zum Lateranconcil 649: Ein zweiter Beitrag zur Dionysius Frage," *Jahresbericht des öffenlichen Privatgymnasiums an der Stelle matutina zu Feldkirch* 4 (1895): 3–96.
13 Stiglmayr, "Der sogenannte Dionysius Areopagita und Severus von Antiochien," *Scholastik* 3 (1928): 1–27, 161–89; idem, "Um eine Ehrenrettung des Severus von Antiochen," *Scholastik* 7 (1933): 52–67.
14 István Perczel, "The Earliest Syriac Reception of Dionysius," in *Re-Thinking Dionysius the Areopagite*, eds. Sarah Coakley and Charles M. Stang (Oxford: Wiley-Blackwell, 2009), 28.
15 Henri-Dominique Saffrey, "New Objective Links Between the Pseudo-Dionysius and Proclus," in *Neoplatonism and Christian Thought*, ed. Dominic O'Meara (Albany, NY: State University of New York Press, 1982), 64–65; Paul Rorem, *Pseudo-Dionysius: A Commentary on the Texts and an Introduction to Their Influence* (Oxford: Oxford University Press, 1993), 17–18.
16 For a list of Pseudo-Dionysius identifications see Ronald F. Hathaway, *Hierarchy and the Definition of Order in the Letters of Pseudo-Dionysius: A Study in the Form and Meaning of the Pseudo-Dionysian Writings* (The Hague: Nijhoff, 1969), 31–35; Caroline Canfield Putnam, *Beauty in the Pseudo-Denis* (Washington, DC: Catholic University of America Press, 1960), 97–102; Salvatore Lilla, "Introduzione allo studio dello Ps. Dionigi l'Areopagita," *Augustianum* 22 (1982): 568–71; Suchla, *Dionysius Areopagita*, 24–25. For the most recent attempts to solve the problem of Pseudo-Dionysian identity (mostly revisiting previously proposed suggestions) or suggesting new places for his geographical residency see Paul Gavrilyuk, who argues for Constantinopolitan placement of Pseudo-Dionysius, "Did Pseudo-Dionysius Live in Constantinople?" *Vigiliae Christianae* 62 (2008): 505–14; Rosemary Arthur strongly suggests that Sergius of Reshaina's candidacy should be reconsidered, *Pseudo-Dionysius as Polemicist*, 116–21, 184–87 (cf. Hathaway, *Hierarchy and the Definition of Order*, 23–25); Tuomo Lankila attempts to revitalize the hypothesis of Damascius as the author of the *CD*, "The 'Corpus Areopagiticum' as a Crypto-Pagan Project," *Journal for Late Antique Religion and Culture* 5 (2011): 14–40; and the reflective suggestion of Alexander Golitzin returning to Peter the Iberian as a possible author, *Mystagogy: A Monastic Reading of Dionysius Areopagita*, ed. Bogdan G. Bucur (Collegeville, MN: Liturgical Press, 2013), 399–406, cf. idem, *Et*

8 Introduction

Introibo Ad Altare Dei: The Mystagogy of Dionysius Areopagita: With Special Reference to Its Predecessors in the Eastern Christian Tradition (Thessalonikh: Patriarchikon Idruma Paterikōn Meletōn, 1994), 415–21; see also Michel van Esbroeck, "Peter the Iberian and Dionysius Areopagita: Honigmann's Thesis Revisited," Orientalia Christiana Periodica 59 (1993): 217–27.

17 Copp, Dionysius the Pseudo-Areopagite: Man of Darkness/Man of Light (Lewiston, NY: Edwin Mellen Press, 2007), 27.
18 PG 4:21AC (lines 12–37) and 21D (lines 45–54)—24A.
19 Beate Regina Suchla, "Die Überlieferung des Prologs des Johannes von Skythopolis zum griechischen Corpus Dionysiacum Areopagiticum: Ein weiterer Beitrag zur Überlieferungsgeschichte des CD," Nachrichten der Akademie der Wissenschaften in Göttingen: Philologisch-Historische Klasse 4 (1984): 176–88, cf. idem, ed., Corpus Dionysiacum IV/1: Ioannis Scythopolitani Prologus et Scholia in Dionysii Areopagitae Librum De Divinis Nominibus cum Additamentis Interpretum Aliorum, PTS 62 (Berlin: Walter de Gruyter, 2011), 108–9.
20 English translation of this passage cited from Rorem and Lamoreaux, John of Scythopolis and the Dionysian Corpus, 106.
21 Ramelli, The Christian Doctrine of Apokatastasis: A Critical Assessment from the New Testament to Eriugena (Leiden: Brill, 2013), 707n135.
22 The CD is not free from a significant degree of polemical issues, which is true to any summa-like body of literature. The Areopagitica definitely has its own agenda. However, any attempt to place this agenda directly into the context of ongoing theological controversies of the time or to tie it to a particular geographical location misplaces the focus from the main objective and contents of the corpus to its peripheral aspects, and as such can be misleading.
23 Golitzin, Mystagogy, 399–401.
24 Wear and Dillon, Dionysius the Areopagite and the Neoplatonist Tradition, 131–32.
25 Canfield Putnam, Beauty in the Pseudo-Denis, 97.
26 Golitzin, "Dionysius Areopagita: A Christian Mysticism?" 166.
27 Paul Rorem, "The Uplifting Spirituality of Pseudo-Dionysius," in Christian Spirituality: Origins to the Twelfth Century, eds. Bernard McGinn, John Meyendorff, and Jean Leclercq (New York, NY: Crossroad Publishing, 1985), 133.
28 See Emma C. Clarke, John M. Dillon, and Jackson P. Hershbell, "Introduction," in Iamblichus: De Mysteriis (Atlanta, GA: Society of Biblical Literature, 2003), XXVII–XXXII. Cf. Wear and Dillon, Dionysius the Areopagite and the Neoplatonist Tradition, 132–33.
29 Balthasar, "Denys," in The Glory of the Lord: A Theological Aesthetics, trans. Andrew Louth, Francis McDonagh, and Brian McNeil (New York, NY: Crossroad Publishing, 1984), 2:148–51.
30 On traditions of pseudonymity in antiquity see Josef A. Sint, Pseudonymität im Altertum, ihre Formen und ihre Gründe (Innsbruck: Wagner, 1960); and Wolfgang Speyer, Die literarsche Fälschung im beidnischen und christlischen Altertum (München: C. H. Beck, 1971).
31 DN 4.12 (709B); PTS 33:157.
32 Stephen Gersh, "The Pseudonymity of Dionysius the Areopagite and the Platonic Tradition," in Neoplatonismo Pagano vs Neoplatonismo Christiano: Identità e Intersezioni, eds. Maria di Pasquale and Concetto Martello (Catania, Spain: Cooperative Universitaria Editrece Catanese di Magistero, 2006), 102n7.

33 Acts 17:22–31. Cf. Andrew Louth, *Denys the Areopagite* (London: G. Chapman, 1989), 10–11.
34 Eusebius of Caesarea's *Praeparatio Evangelica* and *Demonstratio Evangelica* are especially noteworthy.
35 John Philoponus, *Prol.* PG 4:24A; the question is attributed to Numenius, cf. Eusebius of Caesarea, *PE* 11.10.14. This closing passage of *Prologus* to the *CD* Suchla attributes to John Philoponus (Suchla, "Die Überlieferung des Prologs des Johannes von Skythopolis," 4:176–88).
36 Rorem and Lamoreaux, *John of Scythopolis and the Dionysian Corpus*, 21.
37 This hypothesis was initially proposed in my book *The Beauty of the Unity and the Harmony of the Whole: The Concept of Theosis in the Theology of Pseudo-Dionysius the Areopagite* (Eugene, OR: Wipf and Stock, 2009), 88–92. However, the particular problem of the authorship of the *Areopagitica* was not the main subject of the book and was treated only in introductory form. The current book significantly revises and expands this thesis.

1 Attempts to justify pseudonymous affiliation

In the midst of the emphasis on Pseudo-Dionysian reliance on predominantly Neoplatonic, therefore the corruptive to authentic Christianity, inspirations that dominated Dionysian research in the twentieth century, some recent Dionysian scholarship presents several defensive attempts to explain the legitimacy of this pseudonymous affiliation. Hans Urs von Balthasar, who closely, although innovatively, followed by William Riordan, views the attribution of this body of works to Dionysius the Areopagite not as intended forgery, but as reflecting a mystically connoted spiritual relationship of the actual author with the historical Dionysius of the first century. Alexander Golitzin, another prominent scholar of the *CD*, even claims to find the deciphering key to the corpus and proposes several original ideas that can explain and justify attribution of the *CD* to nobody else but Dionysius the Areopagite. Native Syrian Christianity and its monastic communities, in his opinion, clashed with the hierarchical structures of the church and this led to the origination and promulgation of the corpus. Charles Stang advances further the legitimation of pseudonymity in a series of quite intriguing propositions. Stang innovatively makes use of apophatic anthropology to demonstrate how writing under an assumed name can be a form of mystical experience that allows for the actual author to identify himself with Dionysius of the first century and at the same time not to lose self-identity, being simultaneously oneself and someone else. Christian Schäfer points out literary importance of the pseudonymous association of the corpus with the Athenian judge. The pseudonymity of the corpus is not forged; it is fictitious.

Hans Urs von Balthasar

Balthasar believes, if one can put aside any bias against the *CD*, this person inevitably arrives at two conclusions:

> First, that this writer [the author of the *CD*], like no other, is "indivisible" and that his person is wholly identified with his work; in other

words, there is nothing "made-up" about him, that he is no "pseudonym" for another. And then, that such power, such radiance of holiness streams forth from this unity of person and work—as the Middle Ages sensed immediately—that he can in no case be regarded as a "forger," not even as a clever "apologist" pulling off a trick.[1]

The integrity of the corpus, for Balthasar, finds the best testimony in the soundness of its influence. Alexander Golitzin proposes a similar argument in the context of the Eastern Christianity.[2] Basically, if the corpus was accepted by Christian tradition then it ought to be considered orthodox. As an orthodox document it cannot be a forgery.

Pseudonymity is presented in the form of a mystical relationship of the actual author with historical Dionysius the Areopagite that transfers the *CD* from the list of Patristic works to the list of pseudepigraphical ones. As Balthasar continues,

> So a monk, dying to the world, assumes the name of a saint, and lives in his encompassing reality; so too the disciples of the great prophets, living centuries later in the tradition of this particular calling and continuing it, unconsciously attribute their own sayings to the founder: and one speaks rightly of a Deutero- and a Trito-Isaiah, but not of Pseudo-Isaiah.[3]

The role of the pseudonym, or rather Deutero-Dionysius the Areopagite, for Balthasar, is just a testimony to this mystical, trance-like, prophetic relationship between the New Testament figure of Dionysius and the actual author of the corpus. Balthasar basically replaces the idea of pseudonymity with pseudepigrapha, as if pseudepigrapha would be less damaging to the anonymous image of the actual author. The only problem with Deutero-Dionysius, of course, unlike with Isaiah, is we know nothing about the writings of the historical one. Neither do we know any specifics of his theological views or insights preserved even in oral tradition. Balthasar's approach does not remove the charge of forgery; it simply legitimizes it. Balthasar's argument, however, makes an effort to preserve not only historicity (mystically presupposed), but also apostolicity, albeit a deutero-one.

William Riordan

Recently William Riordan returns to and endorses Balthasar's proposal. Riordan also intricately elaborates on it from a theological-ecclesial-pneumatological perspective.[4] For the author of the *CD*, according to Riordan, to write a letter to the apostle John from the first-person, without any hesitation implying his personal friendship with the apostle, would be inconceivable if the author would not be under the realization "that God's eternal mode of being implies His total Presence to all beings of all times and places at once."[5] As in God all distinctions between past, present, and future collapse in a certain "permeability" of time, so it does in the mystery and ministry of the Holy Spirit manifested in the life of the Church and its members. "Because their common identity is with and in the whole Body of Christ (He who lives in them and they in Him [Gal 2:20]), these co-members of the Church co-inhabit one another."[6] Thus, the assumption by the anonymous author of Dionysian identity testifies to "the revealing of a very intimate God-given truth regarding his personal mission in the Church."[7] Already underlined by Balthasar himself, some mystical *teleportation* occurs when the actual author of the corpus transcends himself by entering the identity of the Areopagite. In the Areopagite, according to Riordan, he finds "his truest identity" and in "that divinized identity" he in all truthfulness can address himself to the apostle John as his contemporary.[8]

The idea of a trans-temporal fellowship of all members of the church, the living and the dead, as one body of Christ is not unusual in Christian theology: it is the gathering (the ecclesia) of many individuals united by, through, and in Christ. It is Christ who lives in them and they live in Christ. If many can participate or indwell in Christ, and Christ participates and indwells in many, it does not logically lead to participation and indwelling of many in each other in terms of exchanging identities. What unites the many and makes them one is Christ. It is Christ whom they put on. It is not some kind of kaleidoscopic intermingling of identities with an optional feature for mystical re-incarnational telekinesis at the convenience of the Holy Spirit, as in Riordan. In Riordan's case, it would make better sense for the author of the *CD* to write not as the Areopagite, but as one who received his message from the Areopagite through some kind of mystical vision. In Riordan, as in Balthasar, this justification of pseudonymity does not remove the charge of forgery but only legitimizes it.

Alexander Golitzin

Alexander Golitzin, who strongly defends the Christian orthodoxy of the corpus (especially in its Eastern Orthodox monastic context), is one of the most convinced and often convincing supporters of both the Syrian and the monastic milieu of the *CD*. In Syrian monasticism Golitzin finds "the royal key" that unlocks the mystery of the corpus and reasons for pseudonymity of the author.[9] In his view, the *CD* was written to address certain issues related to some Syrian monks who followed specifically Syrian tradition. These monks considered themselves to have a spiritual authority that was above the authority of the ordained clergy, which naturally had disruptive consequences to the sacramental life of the church and its hierarchical structure, and thus caused conflicts. Living in a spiritual and intellectual environment where apocryphal literature was very popular,[10] these monks saw their authority coming directly from "the seers and prophets of old" and viewed themselves as a real link "between this world and the one to come."[11] In conjunction with Messalianism and its open disregard for sacraments, some of them even claimed that it was possible to have a physically accessible vision of the Trinity. This accentuated the clash "between personal charisma and sacramental authority" even further.[12] Therefore, to bring those undisciplined monks to order, the author of the *CD* adopted his "sub-apostolic pseudonym. He wished, simply, to answer appeals to ancient tradition with countervailing antiquity."[13] In the view that these monks were distrustful of Greek philosophy, the anonymous author of the *CD* specifically saw the wisdom of relying on Neoplatonic philosophy to curtail "the subjective experience of ascetic seers,"[14] where his pseudonymous affiliation also found the perfect fit. Overall, this pseudonymity "served to highlight the content rather than the author,"[15] the use of the esoteric and arcane style was only a ploy to match similarly esoteric language of popular apocryphal books used by those monks, while the corpus itself in its substance is "an anti-esoteric work" addressed to wide audience.[16]

We will return to more detailed discussion of Golitzin's emphasis on the monastic and Syrian background of the *CD* later. As far as his understanding of pseudonymity is concerned, appealing to the authority of apostolic times in an attempt to bring undisciplined monks back to order makes good sense. However, it would be rather unconventional to overload these presupposed sub-apostolic writings heavily with explicitly Neoplatonic elements of non-Christian origin and expect that those rebellious and distrustful of Greek philosophy monks would be convinced. Would it not make them more rebellious? Especially in this context, they would see Dionysian pseudonymity as a vicious forgery. Dionysian Neoplatonism is precisely the issue that still fuels the Dionysian question. In this context, Rosemary Arthur, for example, after discussing at length Dionysian Syrian Christianity, in her view not orthodox but Monophysite, in the end doubts that the author of the corpus was Christian at all. As she remarks, "The deliberate use by Dionysius of so much pagan material does not fit the image of an orthodox Father which many scholars strive to demonstrate. Agreement has still to be reached even on whether Dionysius was a Christian, or a pagan pretending to be a Christian."[17] What makes modern commentators come to such conclusions certainly would instigate even stronger rebellion among Syrian monks who viewed anything Hellenistic as incompatible with their expression of Christianity.

There is one more interesting issue related to the Syrian monastic groups and the function of pseudonymous work in appeasing them. The contextualization of these rebellious Syrian monks in Golitzin leads one to assume that monastic audiences to whom the *CD* was addressed, especially those unruly *pneumathoroi* (the Spirit-bearers) of the old Syrian tradition, were more likely speaking Syriac than Greek. Why then would a Syrian Christian address his works to them in Greek?

Finally, Golitzin's own reflectively hypothetical attribution of the corpus to Peter the Iberian, a Georgian-born Monophysite bishop,[18] does not improve, but rather diminishes, his own premises. It presents the *Areopagitica* as the pseudonymous response of a Monophysite bishop to rebellious Syrian monks, written in Greek and saturated with unadulterated aspects of non-Christian Neoplatonism that is defended as one of the major, authentically Christian and orthodox influences on Eastern Orthodoxy.

Charles Stang

Charles Stang makes several intriguing propositions to justify Dionysian pseudonymity.[19] Some aspects of his approach are helpful. However, his argument would significantly benefit if he engaged more with the preceding *Areopagitica* Patristic and Neoplatonic traditions to demonstrate them. Stang claims that the actual author of the *CD* "writes under the name of Dionysius the Areopagite in order to suggest that, following Paul, he will effect a new rapprochement between the wisdom of pagan Athens and the revelation of God in Christ."[20] This perspective on the *CD*, in my opinion, communicates exactly what our mysterious author intended; however, Stang proposes to demonstrate this exclusively through a Pauline reading of the corpus. Pauline literature is understood in a broad, pre-text critical sense in Stang's work.

The affiliation of the corpus with Paul's convert to Christianity naturally brings attention to the use of Pauline literature,[21] but it also can be argued that Paul is only one of the biblical sources of which Pseudo-Dionysius makes extensive use. Someone can with the similar success look for the key to the corpus in Dionysian use of Johannine literature (also taken in its pre-text critical sense), which is no less extensive. Biblical sources, as is amply shown, for example, by Paul Rorem, have a prominent place in the *Areopagitica*.[22] There is probably no book in the Bible that Pseudo-Dionysius would not cite from or make allusions to in one or another form. However, biblical references do not preclude numerous other Patristic and Hellenistic influences.

Where Stang's argument gets enigmatically interesting is in his particular application of apophatic anthropology. Stang borrows the term "apophatic anthropology" from Bernard McGinn and Denys Turner, who introduced it in the context of the analysis of other mystics, "Dionysius' heirs."[23] Stang proposes that in order for human individuals to "solicit union with the 'unknown God' (Acts 17:23)" they "must also become somehow 'unknown.'"[24] This double apophatism corresponds to the mysticism of the *Areopagitica*. The idea of the union implies some sense of common ground between entities that are united. One has to transcend personal self and in a way make the self unknown in order to be united with the Unknown God. The idea of someone losing or transcending him/herself in order to obtain union with God is a common theme in mysticism—both Christian and Neoplatonic. This approach is exceptionally helpful in assessing the mystical experience between a human individual and a transcendent God that might lead to ecstatic union. It can easily be applied to Dionysian mystical theology as Bernard McGinn applied it in the context of John Scottus Eriugena and Meister Eckhart.[25]

Stang advances this approach further. Apophatic theology not only assumes apophatic anthropology, as in Denys Turner,[26] it also assumes a special significance for pseudonymity itself. The practice of pseudonymous writing is in itself "an ecstatic devotional practice in the service of 'unknowing' both God and self."[27] For Stang, the actual author of the *CD* "does not merely sign the name of Dionysius the Areopagite to his writings. He goes much further and literally assumes the identity of this first-century figure."[28] Writing under the assumed name becomes a mystical experience in itself—"writing pseudonymously is itself a third path of unknowing God and self,"[29] some kind of what might be alternatively called *spiritual teleportation*. Stang proceeds in a paradoxical perspective. The actual author of the *Areopagitica* does not simply go outside of himself and assume the spiritual/mystical identity of Dionysius the Areopagite as in Balthasar and Riordan,[30] he still remains situated in the fifth/sixth century as he extensively cites what could be troubling Neoplatonic statements, describes Byzantine rites, and so on. As Stang recaps,

> The author is, in words borrowed from his description of Moses, "neither himself nor someone else," neither the contemplative from Syria who scholars assume him to be nor the Athenian judge under whose name he writes. Like the ecstatic God with whom he seeks to suffer union, as a writer he simultaneously remains where he is and stretches outside himself.[31]

For Stang, this idea of stretching outside himself is not the description of someone's ecstatic mystical experience when one transcends personal self to the degree of losing the sense of it while still retaining personal

16 *Attempts to justify pseudonymous affiliation*

identity, which more likely was what Pseudo-Dionysius meant when he said, "neither himself nor someone else." In other words, in this sort of out-of-body mystical experience, one does not become someone else but simply loses the sense of personal self. For Stang this phrase receives an interesting twist: "Pseudonymous writing renders the self 'neither [entirely] oneself nor [entirely] someone else,' that is to say, somehow both oneself and someone else. In the case of the author of the CD, he is both himself, an anonymous writer from the late fifth or early sixth century, and also someone else—Dionysius the Areopagite."[32] In this case, we might be dealing with a mystical event that is not precisely speaking to an experience of union with God, but a mystical experience of writing under the identity of another person while still being oneself—sort of a *mystical split personality experience*.

This partial mystical teleportation for Stang legitimizes pseudonymity, because the author of the *CD* "literally assumes the identity of this first-century figure." If it also involves the experience of the union with God as the third path to unknown God, we might be dealing with *mystical multiple personality experience*—a mystical rapture into great unknowns that include identities of one-self (the actual author of the *Areopagitica*), God, and Dionysius the Areopagite (via spiritual teleportation of the author of the *CD* into him). At least it is a split personality experience of transcending oneself in order to become Dionysius the Areopagite without losing oneself. It is either the idea of a mystical union with God that is supplemented with idea of mystical union with an allonym, or simply a mystical union with an allonym without simultaneous mystical union with God.

Christian Schäfer

Christian Schäfer proposes one more way to explain the legitimacy of Dionysian affiliation or "the key to a proper interpretation of the CD" as "the methodological acceptance of the literary fiction of reading an author."[33] The pseudonymity itself is fictitious but not forged: "In the Corpus of his writings, 'Dionysius the Areopagite' is not so much the subject that produced them, but one of the topical subjects the writings treat of."[34] I find, this approach exceptionally helpful and in general agreement with my own hypothesis, although Schäfer is still under the spell of an all too powerful acceptance of the affiliation of this corpus with Dionysius the Areopagite (even though literarily projected) that penetrates *all* aspects of the corpus: "The author [of the corpus] is so completely absorbed in his fictitious self that it basically forces an acceptance of this fictitious self upon the interpreter."[35] As I hope becomes more evident later, the general content of the corpus provides so little actual reliance on its affiliation with historical

Dionysius the Areopagite that such an affiliation can be seen as negligible. The intellectual and theological value of the corpus and its influence would not lose any significance if it is read and interpreted without any affiliation with Dionysius of the first century, apart, of course, from any discomfort that is associated with anonymous or pseudonymous works. However, along with Schäfer, I find a literary application of this identity essential to setting the corpus in accurate perspective. It is not so much historical, or even Schäfer's "factual identity,"[36] as the metaphorical attribution of this corpus to Dionysius the Areopagite, which is what was intended, either by the actual author or those who wanted to promote his writings. The *CD* does not try so much to deal with the relationship between pagan philosophy and Christian doctrine as to present them both as beneficial and almost equally important expressions of divine truth.

Balthasar, Riordan, Golitzin, and Stang are still under the widely spread rather than definitely demonstrated spell of the perception of the *CD* in *its initial design* as purposefully projecting the Areopagite's *historical* identity. This perspective, regardless of any benign intentions, still allows seeing and interpreting the *CD* as a forgery. This, perhaps, is less the case with Golitzin, who in his research for the keys to the corpus in a Syrian milieu, understands the Areopagite attribution as some kind of clever maneuver on the part of the author to impress the monks by the apostolic affiliation in order to bring them to discipline. In Golitzin's case it might be more appropriate to speak about impersonating the Areopagite identity than using his name as allonym. Balthasar treats the corpus as pseudepigraphical literature, and reasserts its apostolicity through Deutero-Dionysianism. Riordan, following Balthasar, adds the element of transcendental permeability and a sort of mutual co-indwelling of members of the Church with each other, where the sense of the timeless fellowship might be seen, even though guided by the Holy Spirit, as spiritual teleportation of one individual into another. Stang follows in some aspects the direction introduced by Balthasar even though he attempts to distance himself from Balthasar. He definitely is far more imaginative than Balthasar. He endeavors to explain the pseudonymity as a complex, multidimensional mystical teleportation that also attempts to reconcile the actual author of the corpus and his fifth-/sixth-century context with historical Dionysius of the first century. Schäfer presents a welcome exception. His approach is more consistent with main themes of the *CD* where pseudonymity plays literary, but not historical, significance.

I argue that reliance on Dionysian pseudonymity is not a major theme in the corpus, as it became later in the history of the Pseudo-Dionysian influence. It has important, but peripheral, and mostly literary, significance that does not attempt to situate the corpus in the first century; rather, the corpus purposefully addresses issues closely contextualized in its immediate fifth-/sixth-century

18 *Attempts to justify pseudonymous affiliation*

environment. This is why our mysterious author quite openly cites Patristic and Neoplatonic sources that easily can jeopardize his *supposedly* first-century identity. Before engaging the overview of what usually is seen as a portrayal of the first-century environment in the *CD*, several other issues should be discussed, as they provide important contextualization of modern scholarship addressing the authorship of the corpus.

Notes

1 Balthasar, "Denys," 2:147.
2 Alexander Golitzin, "The Mysticism of Dionysius Areopagita: Platonist or Christian?" *Mystics Quarterly* 19 (1993): 110–11.
3 Balthasar, "Denys," 2:151.
4 William Riordan, *Divine Light: The Theology of Denys the Areopagite* (San Francisco, CA: Ignatius Press, 2008), 29–34.
5 Riordan, *Divine Light*, 29.
6 Riordan, *Divine Light*, 31.
7 Riordan, *Divine Light*, 33. Riordan's approach is somewhat similar to, but not identical with, that of Charles Stang, which is discussed later in this chapter.
8 Riordan, *Divine Light*, 33–34. What represented the divinizing aspect of this identity transfer is not clear.
9 Golitzin, "Dionysius Areopagita: A Christian Mysticism?" 174–80.
10 Golitzin specifically points out *The Gospel of Thomas*, *The Ascension of Isaiah*, and *The Acts of Judas Thomas*.
11 Golitzin, "Dionysius Areopagita: A Christian Mysticism?" 177.
12 Golitzin, *Et Introibo Ad Altare Dei*, 357. Cf. Arthur, *Pseudo-Dionysius as Polemicist*, 129–36.
13 Golitzin, "Dionysius Areopagita: A Christian Mysticism?" 178.
14 Golitzin, "Dionysius Areopagita: A Christian Mysticism?" 179.
15 The point to which we will return in the context of the main thesis of this monograph.
16 Golitzin, "Dionysius Areopagita: A Christian Mysticism?" 178–79n55.
17 Arthur, *Pseudo-Dionysius as Polemicist*, 143.
18 Golitzin, *Mystagogy*, 399–406. Cf. idem, *Et Introibo Ad Altare Dei*, 415–21.
19 Charles Stang, "Dionysius, Paul and the Significance of the Pseudonym," in *Re-Thinking Dionysius the Areopagite*, 11–25. He repeats his arguments for Dionysian pseudonymity almost verbatim in "'Being Neither Oneself Nor Someone Else': The Apophatic Anthropology of Dionysius the Areopagite," in *Apophatic Bodies*, eds. Chris Boesel and Catherine Keller (New York, NY: Fordham University Press, 2010), 69–71; for fuller exposition of his thesis see his published dissertation, *Apophasis and Pseudonymity in Dionysius the Areopagite: "No Longer I"* (Oxford: Oxford University Press, 2012).
20 Stang, "Dionysius, Paul and the Significance of the Pseudonym," 12.
21 Cf. Golitzin, *Et Introibo Ad Altare Dei*, 234–42.
22 See, for example, Paul Rorem, *Biblical and Liturgical Symbols Within the Pseudo-Dionysian Synthesis* (Toronto: Pontifical Institute of Mediaeval Studies, 1984); and Rorem's footnotes and "Index to Biblical Allusions and Quotations" in English translation of the *CD*.

23 Stang, "Dionysius, Paul and the Significance of the Pseudonym," 23 endnote 4.
24 Stang, "Dionysius, Paul and the Significance of the Pseudonym," 12.
25 Bernard McGinn, *The Growth of Mysticism: Gregory the Great Through the 12th Century* (New York, NY: Crossroad Publishing, 1994), 105–6; idem, "The Negative Element in the Anthropology of John the Scot," in *Jean Scot Érigène et l'histoire de la philosophie: Actes du II Colloque international Jean Scot Erigène*, ed. René Roques (Paris: Éditions du Centre national de la recherche scientifique, 1977), 315–25; idem., *The Mystical Thought of Meister Eckhart* (New York, NY: Crossroad Publishing, 2001), 48.
26 Denys Turner, *The Darkness of God: Negativity in Christian Mysticism* (Cambridge: Cambridge University Press, 1995), 6.
27 Stang, "Dionysius, Paul and the Significance of the Pseudonym," 12.
28 Stang, *Apophasis and Pseudonymity in Dionysius the Areopagite*, 3.
29 Stang, "Dionysius, Paul and the Significance of the Pseudonym," 22.
30 Balthasar, "Denys," 2:151; Riordan, *Divine Light*, 29–34.
31 Stang, "Dionysius, Paul and the Significance of the Pseudonym," 21.
32 Stang, "Dionysius, Paul and the Significance of the Pseudonym," 22 (brackets are in the original).
33 Christian Schäfer, *Philosophy of Dionysius the Areopagite: An Introduction to the Structure and the Content of the Treatise on the Divine Names* (Boston, MA: Brill, 2006), 163.
34 Schäfer, *Philosophy of Dionysius the Areopagite*, 170.
35 Schäfer, *Philosophy of Dionysius the Areopagite*, 170.
36 Schäfer, *Philosophy of Dionysius the Areopagite*, 21, 169.

2 Known and conventionally accepted facets of the *CD* in relation to its authorship

Without a doubt, the *Areopagitica* is enveloped in a cloud of uncertainties and possesses enchanted qualities that dramatically increase its appeal. At the same time, there are several things related to the identity of the author we know with certainty. There also are several issues commonly discussed in Dionysian scholarship in relation to the identity of the author that are often portrayed as conventional knowledge that are not known with certainty. Some of those *knowns* and *unknowns* pertain to the argument proposed here.

The first and the most certain thing about the corpus, and the most obvious at that, is that Dionysius from the first century did not write these treatises. The second important aspect about the *Areopagitica* is the integrity of the corpus itself. From its first recorded introduction in the sixth century the corpus always consisted of the same number of closely related and internally integrated works that came from one historical period and seemingly produced by the single author. The third almost absolutely certain thing about the corpus is that it was written in Greek. As far as the author's native geographical (presumably Syrian) and educational (presumably Athenian) backgrounds are concerned, even though they are often accepted as conventional knowledge about the author of the *CD*, their importance in the context of the authorship is less significant and certain than generally thought.

The fourth definite thing about the corpus is the presence of Neoplatonic influence that cannot be denied. It leads to the fifth certified fact about the *CD*—the presence of Christian content. The presence of both Neoplatonic and Christian material in the corpus often led to strong polarization of opinions dividing modern scholarship. Pseudo-Dionysius is either criticized as a Neoplatonic wolf in Christian clothing, or apologetically defended as an authentic Christian who has almost nothing to do with Neoplatonism. As the consequence, some studies make predominant emphasis on exclusively the Neoplatonic content, while other studies emphasize the Christian content. In both cases it is usually done at the expense of the other. There is a hope that the hypothesis proposed in this monograph—and several most recent Dionysian studies have already begun moving in this direction—can help to bring a needed balance to this polarization and see the *CD* for what it is: the work of a Neoplatonic Christian. The final, the sixth, certain fact, about the *CD* is its tremendous influence on Christian thought and spirituality.

I. Dionysius the Areopagite mentioned in the Book of Acts is not the author

The first important known fact about the *CD* is that the Dionysius the Areopagite mentioned in the Book of Acts is not the author. This is the most obvious statement, but this also is the most certain thing about the *Areopagitica*. Even after Koch and Stiglmayr conclusively established the pseudonymous nature of the corpus, it did not silence those voices defending the actual Dionysian authorship.[1] Today, it is probably the only aspect of the corpus where everybody agrees.

Although Dionysius the Areopagite is not the author, what is important is that the actual author of the corpus made his ideas public, where the affiliation of these works with the Areopagite might have important metaphorical significance. Regardless of the complexity of his concepts and idiosyncrasy of his turgid style overloaded with neologisms and repetitions he wrote and published his works. What was and remains hidden are not his ideas, but his identity. Considering that his anonymity was intended, in light of the proposed hypothesis of assigning this corpus to Dionysius the Areopagite as a literary ploy, it is possible to come to the conclusion that by providing this literary attribution the author made use of a clever rhetorical trick to amplify the effect of his ideas without any malicious implication to introduce these works as belonging to the first century. Who would not want to read the works of the otherwise unknown Areopagite even if these writings represent their ascription metaphorically? This serves as an external factor of literary application. The internal relevance of this literary application is extremely intriguing and closely connected with the so-called Dionysian society. It will be addressed in Chapter Four.

II. The integrity of the corpus

The integrity of the corpus is another generally acknowledged fact regarding the *Areopagitica*. There is a unique identity of the content that is associated with the *CD* as a whole, both external (the number of works that compose the corpus) and internal (their mutual interdependency and ascription to the pen of one author). There is, at least, one dissenting voice regarding the single author theory. Rosemary Arthur without further detailed elaboration suggests that "the corpus was written in a hurry by more then [*sic.*] one person and inadequately edited."[2] It is probably true that the *CD* was hastily written, and there is some ground to suggest that it was poorly edited; however, it is unlikely that the *Areopagitica* was a group project. At the same time, being a work of single author does not rule out the possibility of some additional editorial work or interpolations. This, nevertheless, does not have significant impact on the integrity of the text and its perception throughout Christian tradition.

From their first introduction, throughout the Middle Ages, the Renaissance, and up to the present, the collection of Pseudo-Dionysian writings always consisted of four treatises (*The Divine Names*, *The Mystical Theology*, *The Celestial Hierarchy*, *The Ecclesiastical Hierarchy*) and ten letters that appear to be written by one person.[3] The theological treatises constitute a unified, mutually complementary exposition, while the letters are "an integral part of the *Corpus* as a whole."[4] The collection of these writings was never expanded or reduced. None of these writings were assigned to different periods, nor their belonging to the corpus ever questioned.[5] This is in spite of the fact that the corpus itself makes claims to be a larger body of works than what we have since its first known appearance.

In addition to what now consists of the *Areopagitica*, Pseudo-Dionysius among his other works mentions *The Symbolic Theology*,[6] *The Theological Representations* (*The Theological Outlines*),[7] *On the Properties and Ranks of the Angels*,[8] *On the Soul*,[9] *Concerning Justice and the Judgment of God*,[10] *On the Divine Hymns*,[11] and *The Conceptual and the Perceptible* (*The Intelligible and the Sensible*).[12] Besides being mentioned and occasionally outlined by Pseudo-Dionysius, there are no surviving manuscripts of these works. These writings are neither referred to nor cited by anybody else outside of the *CD*. We also possess no extant fragments of them. Louth, following Roques, makes a suggestion that references to these otherwise unknown or lost works might be part of a ploy to create the impression "that the works we have were all that survived to the end of the fifth century of a much larger corpus of writings written at the end of the first."[13] Balthasar dismisses any possible "mystification" and believes that, at least some of these works were actually written, while others could be designed in the mind of the author. He thinks that the extant and lost works are essential for an overall understanding of the Dionysian structure of theology.[14]

Recently, tracing the earliest Syriac reception of the *CD*, István Perczel made a suggestion that can collaborate Balthasar's opinion, although with an additional turn. Perczel points out that the first translator of the corpus into Syriac, Sergius of Reshaina, might have had firsthand knowledge of some now-lost works of Pseudo-Dionysius.[15] According to Perczel, in his introduction to the translation Sergius mentions *The Theological Representations* and *The Symbolic Theology* while not distinguishing between lost and extant works, "For Sergius, ... these 'lost' works constitute organic parts of the systematic doctrinal exposition that he credits to Dionysius."[16] Nevertheless, Sergius translates only what we know as the extant works. Whether Sergius actually read these lost works or simply relied on what Pseudo-Dionysius revealed about them in his extant works Perczel does not know, but he thinks "that they were not 'lost', but simply published under *different* pseudonyms."[17] Why that might be the case remains unclear. Stang raises several reasonable objections:

> If, as Perczel argues, the author of the CD published the 'lost' works under different pseudonyms, then why in the CD, when he is writing under the name of Dionysius, does he refer to those works as his own? Furthermore, if Sergius knew that both the CD and the 'lost' works were all composed by the same author, why would he draw on the whole body of literature for his introduction but then translate only the CD?[18]

Of course, if Sergius was the actual author of the *Areopagitica* he would have more freedom to refer to whatever he might think is useful and appropriate in the translation of his own works, while using the translation as a clever cover to avoid unnecessary exposure.[19]

There are at least two exceptions to the claim that the existence of lost treatises is fictitious. The first is the recent attention given to one poetic work *Hymn to God* (Ὕμνος εἰς θεόν).[20] This hymn initially was attributed to Gregory of Nazianzus; however, Gregory's authorship was dubious for a long time, until it was entirely discarded by Albert Jahn in 1891, who suggested Proclus as the possible author.[21] Almost 100 years later Sicherl proposed Pseudo-Dionysius as a potential author of the text.[22] Henri-Dominique Saffrey agrees with Sicherl.[23] Was *Hymn to God* written by the mysterious author of the *Areopagitica* or not? We do not really know, although his authorship might be plausible and is supported by internal evidence in his surviving works.

Perczel suggests another exception. He believes that he discovered one of the lost Dionysian works, *The Theological Representations*, as *De trinitate*, erroneously attributed to Didymus the Blind. The points of connection between *De trinitate* and the *CD* are that both utilize the same passages from Proclus.[24]

While the these proposals are engaging, they still are not conclusive. Were the otherwise unknown works of Pseudo-Dionysius mentioned in the corpus simply fictitious, lost, or never written? We do not know. Nevertheless, the integrity of the corpus as it came to us from the sixth century remains remarkably intact. This fact, in the light of the main hypothesis of this book, is important because it shows that the literary attribution to Dionysius the Areopagite is consistent with the holistic and premeditated literary design of the corpus. It is not a collection of works written by one author for different purposes, like, for example, Augustine's *Confessions* and *On the Trinity*, but one body of works internally interconnected to express specific thematic homogeneity. The premeditated design of the corpus might also include non-extant or never-written treatises to serve important purpose. The literary idea behind the non-extant works that are mentioned in the corpus presents Dionysius the Areopagite as the first after Origen, in a quite modern as well as a Medieval scholastic sense, systematic theologian and visionary. The combination of extant and referenced treatises creates a sense of the projection of a detailed and complete system of Christian theology and worldview. As some non-extant works are only mentioned, others are discussed and their contents are summarized. In all instances, with the titles of these works or summaries of their contents, the author might be attempting to indicate the compatibility of what we find in the extant works with other less debatable and commonly known topics of Christian theology. By doing so, he diminishes what some might see as novelty by simply narrating or contextualizing them into seemingly traditional Christian perspective. All key aspects of Christian theology are acknowledged in the *Areopagitica*, but not all of them are discussed with proper diligence. However, the *idea* of this diligent discussion is communicated by references to other works.

As far as the extant works are concerned, even taken by themselves their internal integrity is harmoniously interconnected with their contents and main objective themes of the corpus. In opinion of Bernard McGinn, "*DN* is primarily concerned with procession, whereas *EH* and *CH* deal with lower stages of reversion. *MT* completes the account of reversion and concludes by saying what little can be said about God in himself through a series of supereminent expressions."[25] The Letters serve best as an Introduction.[26]

III. Geographical provenance and linguistic preference

The Syrian, supposedly monastic, background and Athenian Neoplatonism, which is closely associated with Proclus, are often accepted as the most obvious and rarely questioned features of the corpus.[27] Introduction of the corpus to wider circulation by Severus of Antioch made the Syrian and, it can be added, Monophysite affiliation of the corpus the most obvious guess. Stiglmayr even proposed Severus as a possible author.[28] However, without necessarily denying the possibility of the Syrian upbringing of our anonymous author, it is hard to establish with certainty what exactly makes the *CD exclusively* a Syrian product. There is no lack of proposals; at the same time, their results are not so assuring. It is also important to point out that the author of the *Areopagitica* never hinted that he knew Syriac or that he was a Syrian.

Alexander Golitzin, as we have already mentioned, with overwhelming energy insists on a Syrian and monastic connection for the actual author.[29] He is true to his statement: "I must confess that I am nearly unique in drawing attention to the later [Syrian Christian background in the *Areopagitica*], and quite unique in stressing it as I do."[30] In his opinion, our mysterious author is so deeply rooted in Syrian Christianity that "Christian Syria, in short, supplies a vital and up to now entirely missing piece in the puzzle not only of Dionysius' Christian background but as well both of his swift reception and of the great authority that he would enjoy in the Christian East ever afterwards."[31] Golitzin allows for the presence of some apologetic design in the corpus: sort of an apologetic effort to present Christianity in a more or less acceptable and convincing way to non-Christian intellectuals.[32] The main significance of the *CD* for Golitzin, however, is to reconcile "the occasionally clashing claims of bishops and monks, of liturgy and mysticism."[33] Golitzin also highlights a Dionysian challenge to the Origenist controversy in Syria-Palestine. This aspect of his research, however, does not address any specific issues related to pseudonymity, with only one exception. In both instances (apologetic inclinations and anti-Origenist thrust), the proposed Syrian identity of the author and his familiarity with Syrian monastic tradition remains intact and above reproach. Only Syrian Christianity shapes for Golitzin the main framework of the *Areopagitica*. Even more, the influence that comes from the ascetic literature of his native Syrian Christianity prevails over the reliance on Iamblichus and Proclus.[34] In other words, for Golitzin, the influence that comes from the ascetic literature of his native Syrian Christianity supersedes by far the influence of Neoplatonism.

Obviously, there is no reason to deny the influence of the *Areopagitica* on Eastern Orthodox spirituality and monasticism, including Syrian Christianity of post-Dionysian times. It also is possible that this corpus had some Syrian monastic audience in mind, but this is far from being conclusive. The persuasiveness of Golitzin's style, and the originality of his argumentation, creates a truly convincing effect on the reader. Golitzin effectively manages to uncover elements of Syrian background that seem to find direct correlation with the text of the *Areopagitica*. Often, however, it is done by somewhat superficial juxtaposition of Syrian and Dionysian texts, where through supposed similarities between them the direct connection is proclaimed. The basic reading of the Dionysian text—after reading some of Golitzin's interpretations of it—often makes the certainty of Golitzin's propositions look less certain. From conditionally structured statements Golitzin commonly jumps to categorically affirmative ones. By the abundance of extensive referencing to all kinds of sources (overpowering most of his writing) and through affirmative, presented as proven, propositions (sometimes without equally clear and balanced argumentation), Golitzin appears to paint a persuasive picture of his approach. Nevertheless, the things he omits or only mentions in passing without detailed treatment make all of his efforts one sided and often biased.

There is some rhetorical quality to Golitzin's argumentation. Looking exclusively at the list of uncovered Syrian elements and their cleverly interpreted presence in the corpus helps to create an impression of significant Syrian influence. The truth to be told, a similar effect can be achieved by concentrating on expressly Neoplatonic references to claim an exclusively Neoplatonic character for the *CD*. Concentrating exclusively on Pauline references, one could come to see exclusively Pauline influence in the corpus. The reality is that the number of references to Syrian Christianity that Golitzin uncovers are comparatively less abundant in the text than he makes the reader to believe, and they yield to more easily detectable and more abundant Neoplatonic and Greek Patristic material.

Golitzin does not deny Neoplatonic elements of the corpus; he suggests that they have already been sufficiently, even excessively, addressed by other scholars, so he generally bypasses any detailed discussions of them and concentrates the bulk of his research on exclusively Christian and orthodox aspects, especially in their Eastern Orthodox monastic and liturgical contextualization.[35] However, even as far as Syria-Palestine is concerned, the presence of Hellenistic culture there should not be downplayed. Many Christian intellectuals of the fifth and sixth centuries were from this large geographical area, including John of Scythopolis, the first major commentator on the *Areopagitica*, who wrote in Greek and were known for their familiarity with Hellenistic learning.

As far as the Christian side of the corpus is concerned, there is greater *Greek* Patristic influence in the *CD* than distinctly *Syrian*. This point inadvertently is apparent from Golitzin's own research. His assessment of Greek Patristic predecessors of our mysterious author of the *Areopagitica* takes roughly 120 pages, while the specifically Syrian aspect is covered in less than 40 pages.[36] Moreover, some allusions, interpreted as specifically Syrian, in their content can be seen as either inconclusive, as far as their influence on the *Areopagitica* is concerned, or too broad. In other words, they can be viewed as either accidental or belonging to Christian tradition in general rather than to specifically its Syrian expression. Several Syrian peculiarities of the corpus can be with the same effectiveness explained from a Greek Patristic background. Besides, we do not find any references or allusions in the *CD* to the apocryphal works that Golitzin pointed out as popular among Syrian monks.[37] Andrew Louth, for instance, also accepts that some part of Dionysian background comes from Syrian Christianity, he especially draws parallels with Ephrem the Syrian and his treatment of divine names. Louth even acknowledges the temptation to see in the evidence even more. However, he remarks, "There are other influences on Denys's treatment of the divine names that seem more important." He specifically refers here to Neoplatonic influence.[38]

With regard to the *CD* addressing issues of monasticism, it is not as certain as sometimes portrayed. It is possible that the author of the *CD* was a monk (there is almost unquestionable consensus about this in recent Pseudo-Dionysian scholarship), likely he also was a priest or even a bishop.[39] Presenting Dionysius the Areopagite as the author, the actual author explicitly makes an impression that this body of works was written by a bishop. This is especially apparent in the introductory part of *EH* where the author exhorts the addressee Timothy to keep the arcane mystagogy of "divinely worked understanding" only for initiated and away from eyes of uninitiated.[40] Truly initiated "sacred men" of the ecclesial hierarchy are bishops as our mysterious author makes clear at the end of the introductory chapter where he again insists on keeping sacred knowledge away from uninitiated: "I am giving you this gift of God, together with other things pertaining to the hierarchs. I do so because of the solemn promises you made, of which I am now reminding you, promises never to pass to anyone except sacred-initiators of your own order of the hierarch's superior sacred words."[41] The following description of Christian sacraments and their meaning also is presented from the perspective of a bishop or a hierarch. At the same time the clerical status of the presumed or the actual author is not that self-evident in the text. The subtitle "presbyter" writing to "fellow-presbyter" used in the *CD* in works addressed to Timothy is confusing. If Timothy, who according to Eusebius was the first bishop of Ephesus,[42] along with the proposed author of the corpus are called presbyters in order to mimic the New Testament environment where the term "presbyter" can be used interchangeably with "bishop" than why are the addressees of *Ep.* 7 and 9 addressed as hierarchs, a title certainly not attested in the New Testament? The whole outline of the ecclesial hierarchy in the *CD* would make more sense to correlate presbyter (πρεσβύτερος) with priest (ἱερεύς), and bishop (ἐπίσκοπος) with hierarch (ἱεράρχης). Only subtitles to the *Areopagitica*'s epistles seem to follow these ecclesiastical ranks consistently.

In some sense the vocabulary preference for "presbyter" or even lower ranking designations in subtitles might be done on purpose as, by the time of the *CD*'s public appearance, some of the most prominent writers were not bishops, but members of lower clergy. Leontius of Byzantium, Leontius of Jerusalem, and Maximus the Confessor are good examples. Needless to mention that some figures closely related to the *Areopagitica* such as

28 Conventionally accepted facets of the CD

John Philoponus, one of early commentators on the corpus, and Sergius of Reshaina, the first translator of the CD into Syriac, were prominent intellectuals and theologians who might not even belong to the clergy. There is some possibility that Sergius was a presbyter, but his known occupation was a physician. The clerical status of John Philoponus is uncertain. Reference to Philoponus as the bishop of Alexandria is more likely a case of mistaken identity, where he was confused with John of Alexandria who actually anathematized him in 575.[43] Several Byzantine emperors, lay people by their ecclesiastical standing, also were actively involved in church affairs as theologians.

The mixture of Neoplatonic and Christian ideas in the CD can indicate that the author might not be a bishop or even a monastic in real life. The mechanical schematism of the EH might even indicate that the actual author, who certainly was intimately familiar with the sacramental and liturgical life of the church, was not thoroughly concerned with the ecclesiastical structure of the church. Thus, there is no less probability that he could be an ascetically living, non-monastic individual, perhaps a philosophically minded priest, who was actually not attempting to reform monasticism but rather was resisting the growing influence of monasticism, especially in its militant form.[44] As far as monastic life is concerned, Louth correctly points out that the CD is concerned with only one theme: "The monk is a single-minded pursuer of union with unity or the One.... We hear nothing of rules or communities or abbots or superiors or of obedience—all an important part of monasticism as Denys would have known it."[45] Louth, however, indicates that the single-mindedness emphasized in the CD might refer to special forms of Syrian monastic groups, perhaps the same ones that Golitzin has in mind. In Louth, this does not become the key to the corpus and does not go beyond historical observation, while in Golitzin it becomes the most missed aspect of Dionysian scholarship. Golitzin seems to rely in part on Louth's observation to develop his own, more speculative, and hence less historically grounded, version.[46]

The CD projects the idea of a multidimensional, sacredly designed understanding of universal and social orders, including apophatic contemplative orientation, but its philosophically minded ontological and metaphysical aspects dominate over exclusively monastic ones. It certainly does not preclude some monastic individuals or communities from philosophizing, but the corpus seems better situated in an ascetically oriented, but not necessarily monastic, environment. Even if the author of the CD was a Syrian, he was a highly Hellenized Syrian who would have more affinity for the Neoplatonic elite than the distinct native features of Syrian Christianity. Pseudo-Dionysius is not any less a Christian than he is a Neoplatonist. The ideals of ascetic and contemplative life actually congenially come together for both traditions. Besides, with all the inspiring attraction of these writings there is also a sense of an almost artificially imposed implementation of Proclian triadic principle that is more reflective of certain popular *academic* patterns of the time rather than congenial with explicitly Syrian Christian pronouncements. This "ecclesiastical scholasticism," to borrow Harnack's expression,[47] of the hierarchy of angelic beings and the transmission of divine knowledge not directly from God to human beings but through the intermediacy of their ranks is a good example. To argue otherwise would make the Athenian Neoplatonism look like the central theme of indigenous Syrian Christianity.

As far as Golitzin's argument for an essentially Eastern Orthodox reading of the *Areopagitica*, considered in the light of his insistence of a rather frozen-in-time ideal state of Orthodox spirituality, "largely unaltered since the Byzantine Middle Age,"[48] as necessary for a proper understanding and authentic appropriation of the corpus, is an anachronistic argument. It also inadvertently might imply that certain aspects of Eastern Orthodoxy simply lacked any significant theological development since their Middle Age Byzantine expression. As insightful as they might be, they would constitute a stagnation of Eastern Orthodox tradition that did not have any important and relevant application beyond Gregory Palamas. The fact that the *CD* significantly influenced and shaped Eastern Orthodoxy does not diminish the presence of non-Christian Neoplatonic content in of the corpus.

Rosemary Arthur also strongly supports the Syrian identity of Pseudo-Dionysius; however, she is more critical than Golitzin of our mysterious author's Christianity. She finds him a Monophysite who was writing in response to the crisis within Monophysitism due to theological and, mostly, political pressures, including tensions among different Monophysite groups.[49] Arthur presents a well-researched account of Syrian sources that might have had influence on our anonymous author, especially in his treatment of the angelic world. However, her findings lead her to less assuring results. She admits that the overall extent to which the Syrian background is present in the *CD* is quite limited.[50] Even in her assessment of possible appropriation of Syrian angelic material she arrives at conflicting results—our anonymous author is independent from and "in marked contrast to the contemporary Syrian attitude."[51] Apparently, while being a Syrian, Pseudo-Dionysius does not engage significantly with his native milieu. This is not to suggest he was not a Syrian, but Pseudo-Dionysius manifests more reliance on a Greek Patristic heritage than on a specifically Syrian one.

As far as Athenian Neoplatonism is concerned, first, this form of Neoplatonism is not specifically an inherent feature of Syrian Christianity. This is not to say that anything Neoplatonic is absent in anything Syrian,[52] but it can hardly be the most central theme of native Syrian Christianity. Second

30 *Conventionally accepted facets of the CD*

and importantly, differences between the Athenian and Alexandrian Neoplatonic schools should not be exaggerated. As Richard Wallis notes: "Relations between the two schools were always close and intermarriage between their members common. . . . Moreover, many Neoplatonists taught in both cities, or at least studied in one before going on to teach in the other."[53] Furthermore, the eventual passing of the Alexandrian Neoplatonic School to Christian management, together with a long-standing Christian intellectual tradition, presents Alexandria as one of the fertile grounds for such works as the *CD*. My personal inclination is to see Alexandria as a place where the *Areopagitica* originated. The Alexandrian Neoplatonic School had a different and more cooperative (not without tensions) relationship between its pagan and Christian members—in other words it was not so pronouncedly pagan in its Neoplatonic perspective as the Athenian Academy. The influence of Origen with all related speculative aspects of Christian thought along with strong monastic traditions, both in their positively influential spirituality and their possibly condemned (or at least referred in the *CD*) militancy, and the almost totalitarian form of hierarchical control (well attested in Alexandria) also point to this city. In the absence of solid historical evidence, an Alexandrian location for the corpus becomes plausible, but cannot be definitely ascertained.

One also should not underestimate the mobility available in the Roman Empire. A Syrian, Palestinian, or Constantinopolitan Christian could easily study in Athens or Alexandria, if one chose and had the means to do so. The student body and the faculty in Late Antiquity were represented by a quite ethnically and religiously diverse group of individuals. Prominent Christian fathers Basil of Caesarea and Gregory of Nazianzus, natives of Cappadocia, received their education in Athens. Gregory of Nazianzus reflecting on his experience in Athens explicitly confirms his appreciation for the city as "the home of eloquence, Athens, a city to me, if to anyone, truly golden, patroness of all that is excellent."[54] The teacher of the non-Christian Eunapius in Athens was a Christian sophist, the Armenian Prohaeresius, who during the reign of Emperor Julian was prohibited from teaching.[55] A certain Diophantus, teacher of Libanius, "was a native of Arabia who forced his way into the ranks of the professors of rhetoric."[56] John Chrysostom, possibly, studied with pagan Libanius in Antioch.[57] Apparently, in the educational environment as well as in cultural environment among intellectual elite in Late Antiquity there was no strict pagan–Christian divide. What all of them had in common was the Hellenistic culture.

There, however, should be noted one more detail that might signify the importance of associating the *CD* with specifically Athenian Neoplatonism. Polymnia Athanassiadi proposes the northern slope of the Areopagus as the place where the last Diadochus of the Athenian Academy, Damascius, transferred the Academy's campus.[58] If the author of the *CD* was in some capacity, either as a student or perhaps as a teacher, affiliated with the Academy under the leadership of Damascius, who became a head by 515,[59] he legitimately could call himself the Areopagite. And *if his name happened to be Dionysius, he actually wrote under his own name*. Unfortunately, we do not know anyone under this name in the last days of the Academy. Nevertheless, if the final days of the Academy transpired on the Areopagus it might suggest important literary significance that would not be missed by immediate contemporaries. The association of the corpus with Dionysius the Areopagite of the first century, Pauline convert to Christianity, brings to mind Athens. The last Academy's residence that Damascius in the sixth century housed on the Areopagus connects it with Neoplatonism. It is a symbolic identification of the proposed author of the corpus with the last geographical location of the Athenian Academy, meeting place of the beginning of Christianity at Athens and the conclusion of Neoplatonic teaching there. In this case, the Areopagus affiliation signifies some sense of congeniality between Christianity, in the name of the proposed author of the *CD*, and Hellenistic philosophy, in the place of its final days, and might also imply the author's regret about the drastic repressive measures of the Emperor Justinian in closing the Academy in 529. Otherwise, the particular geographical location of the Neoplatonic content of the corpus, in spite of its close connection to the philosophy of Proclus, cannot be precisely identified.

As the geographical, ethnic, and educational whereabouts of Pseudo-Dionysius are still debatable, what is certain is that Pseudo-Dionysius *wrote in Greek*. Arthur in passim suggests that some peculiarities or anomalies of Dionysian Greek can be explained as a result of Greek not being his native language.[60] Thomas Campbell, who also thinks that Pseudo-Dionysius was a Monophysite Christian "though not heretical," finds "at once Attic and barbaric" language of our mysterious author as a possible indication that Greek was not his native language. He endorses a proposal that Peter the Iberian, native of Georgia, might be an actual author of the corpus.[61] Even if this is the case, which is highly probable, Dionysian knowledge of Greek Patristic and Neoplatonic literature and terminology betrays that he learned it in Greek, and also indicates quite profound Greek proficiency.[62]

Curiously enough, even Golitzin, after insistent promotion of a *native* and *orthodox* Syrian background for our anonymous author, suggestively proposes Peter the Iberian,[63] Georgian-born Monophysite bishop of Maiuma (a town near Gaza), as a possible author of the corpus.[64] Thus, Golitzin, perhaps unintentionally, points to a rather cosmopolitan exchange of cultural and educational backgrounds where what might signify the intellectual identity of the *Areopagitica* does not necessarily rely on any particular geographical or ethnic affiliation. The overarching Hellenistic cultural environment still remains the main culprit.

The fact that Pseudo-Dionysius wrote in Greek is significant for several reasons. The first is the most obvious. Dionysius the Areopagite, the Athenian judge, as proposed author of these works cannot produce them in any other language. This reflects not only the literary ploy employed in the corpus but is also closely connected with the cultural and intellectual influence of the corpus, its influence on the formation of imperial Byzantine Christian identity. The *Areopagitica* among many others things is the product of Hellenistic intellectual culture.

Christianity from the beginning did not really find itself in total opposition to, nor was it entirely ostracized from, the Hellenistic culture. The Greek language of the New Testament is a good testimony that from the beginning Christianity was situated in the Hellenistic world. Furthermore, influence of the predominantly Platonic tradition with its variety of expressions became a deeply integrated part of Christian discourse a long time before the fifth or sixth century. However, Christian appropriation of Platonic terminology and paradigmatic forms of expression should not be seen as simple borrowing from Platonism. It is not an uncommon cultural and intellectual development when someone is influenced and utilizes the philosophical patterns of thinking that are dominating this person's cultural surroundings, to the degree that those patterns are not perceived to be in conflict with personal beliefs.[65] The language of Platonism was the common medium for any intellectual exchange of the time.

Looking for a specific geographical location or ethnic background of the author as the right key to unlock the mystery of the *CD* might be an intriguing, even exciting detective experience, but one that can lead only to speculative or, at best, inconclusive results. They are of secondary importance as far as the main influence of this corpus is concerned. Whoever the author of the *CD* was, Byzantine, Syrian, or Coptic, one thing is certain: he wrote in Greek extensively utilizing both Christian and Neoplatonic vocabulary and concepts. Unprecedented before Pseudo-Dionysius, the incorporation of Neoplatonism and Christianity is the most significant and apparent influence of this corpus throughout the centuries, and is key to its role in the formation of imperial Christian identity.

IV. Pseudo-Dionysius as Neoplatonic philosopher

The indebtedness of the *CD* to Neoplatonism is commonly acknowledged. Eric Perl (among others) recently demonstrated the organic relation of Dionysian philosophy with Neoplatonic philosophical foundations, especially Plotinus and Proclus.[66] Dionysian understanding of the super-transcendence of God or the One who is beyond being, as well as his understanding of causality, metaphysical stratification, mystical union, the dynamics of remaining-procession-return, evil as privation, the process of purification-illumination-perfection, and his particular triadic and enneadic arrangement of hierarchies cannot be properly assessed apart from Neoplatonism. Perl, in his comprehensive analysis, not only manages to increase appreciation for Pseudo-Dionysius as a philosopher, but he also interprets Neoplatonism from a new and refreshing perspective.

Pseudo-Dionysius is not simply subservient to Neoplatonic learning; he actually contributes to the development of Neoplatonism. As Wear and Dillon remark:

> One notable feature of the Dionysian corpus is the extravagant and hyperbolic use of language that greets one on every page. It is plainly part of Dionysius' project to outdo the Hellenistic philosophers in an area in which they would particularly pride themselves, the use of technical terminology. Dionysius not only adopts much of the characteristic terminology of the fifth-century Platonic Academy of Athens; he repeatedly 'trumps' it by devising new terms and compounds of his own, and, in some notable cases, by employing a philosophical term in a new sense.[67]

The author of the *CD* was so intimately acquainted with Neoplatonism that he arguably can be identified as a Neoplatonic philosopher himself. In other words, even apart from Christian aspects of Dionysian theology, some of his contributions are merited on exclusively Neoplatonic grounds. Hence it is not surprising that Gersh pointed out some Pseudo-Dionysian impact on Damascius.[68] It is probable that Damascius was a contemporary of Pseudo-Dionysius. At the very least, it is likely that Damascius was familiar with the *CD*. Although the intense anti-pagan campaigns of the sixth century, which had devastating effects on pagan learning institutions and on the pagan countryside, should not be downplayed, there is more to the intellectual dialogue and exchange of ideas between the Christian and pagan educated elite. Pseudo-Dionysius was not the only one who relied on Neoplatonic sources; he was also read within Neoplatonic circles.

V. Pseudo-Dionysius as a church father

The *Areopagitica* is a work of a Neoplatonic mind, but hardly of one who tried to conceal non-Christian Neoplatonism under a Christian façade. It is impossible to deny that the *CD* incorporates a significant amount of scriptural and Patristic material. Often-raised questions are: Was the author of the *CD* a true Christian? How authentic is the Christianity of Pseudo-Dionysius? But these questions only confuse rather than advance a better understanding of the *Areopagitica*. What is authentic Christianity? Is a Roman Catholic an authentic Christian? Or Eastern Orthodox? Or Lutheran? Or Presbyterian? Is an Origenist Christian an authentic one? Or a Monophysite Christian? Or a Chalcedonian Christian? Or a Neoplatonic Christian? Yes, each of them is authentic in its own right. So also is the author of the *CD*. Simply proving that he is dependent on Proclus does not prove that he is a pagan.

At the same time, if anyone attempts to justify the Christian orthodoxy of the *Areopagitica* from the twenty-first-century perspective of any established Christian tradition, it would lead only to disappointing or artificial results. The theological sophistication, philosophical complexity, intended and unintended obscurity, and especially the individual theological preferences and sympathies of the actual author of the *CD* cannot fit perfectly any established form of Christianity, although his work still bears significant influence on Christian heritage, especially in the context of the Eastern Orthodox and Roman Catholic traditions. Even if one only sees in the corpus a purely Neoplatonic work disguised under a Christian façade (especially research that proposes Damascius as the author),[69] the Christian content of the corpus cannot be denied or ignored. In this particular case, the *allegedly pagan* author of the *CD* demonstrates not only intimate familiarity with Christian Scriptures, including some knowledge of Hebrew, but also quite expert knowledge of Christian theology with particular interest in advancing angelology, liturgical sacramentalism, and biblical names of God, as well as expert comprehension of the doctrine of the Trinity.

Dionysian Neoplatonism and Christianity present the intricately intermingled content of the corpus while at the same time leading to the most polarized assessments in modern scholarship. Pseudo-Dionysius is either studied from a predominantly Neoplatonic perspective or from a Christian perspective. The positive side of this polarization is that it demonstrates the value and originality of the corpus contributing to both avenues. On the other hand, this polarization in the fight for either a Neoplatonic or a Christian identity for the mysterious author actually might be one of the major obstacles to appreciating the *Areopagitica* as it is: the genuinely Neoplatonic work of a genuinely Christian author. Nobody in preceding Patristic tradition can supersede Pseudo-Dionysius in the degree of his implementation of Greek philosophy. His reliance on preceding Patristic tradition is no less remarkable. Those two things do not need to be exclusive. It is not either/or; it is both/and. The author of the *Areopagitica* was a Neoplatonic Christian.

Whether as a Christian he was more of a Monophysite, or an Origenist, or an anti-Origenist, or a Chalcedonian is of secondary importance to the actual intention of the author. The corpus has little to no references to the personal experience of the actual author, and seems to be intentionally staying away from theologically controversial debates of the time. This does not mean that the *CD* entirely ignored, for example, the subject of Christology. Christological references are present in the corpus, but they are rather purposefully ambiguous, inconclusive, and inconsequential in assisting to determine the author's theological position. As Louth observes, "The technical Christology of that century has left little imprint on the Areopagitica; indeed part of the reason for his pseudonymity may have been to escape that suffocating world."[70] Pseudo-Dionysius is not, properly speaking, a consistent theologian of Origenist or Monophysite persuasion, nor explicitly Chalcedonian and anti-Origenist. However, this does not mean he is a confused theologian. The sense of confusion might occur if someone tries to associate him with one or another camp of Christian theology assuming that those camps in themselves had homogeneously expressed forms of theology.

As far as the topic of Christology in the corpus is concerned, the lack of an explicit position on the issue, first, indicates that the *Areopagitica* was written in the post-Chalcedonian period, which is to state the obvious. Second, concerns for personal safety should not be ruled out. Most importantly, the understanding of Christ's incarnation as composite of two natures, divine and human, presents certain problems for maintaining the consistency of the Dionysian metaphysical edifice.

By having two different and in some Pseudo-Dionysian sense incompatible or, the least, directly non participatory, realities, Christ simultaneously belongs to the super-transcendent realm of the Thearchy[71] and the ecclesiastical or human hierarchy.[72] From Dionysian ontological and metaphysical presuppositions, this union is problematic as it complicates the smooth flow of the descending chain of divine generation and illumination from God through angelic orders to humanity. Additionally, it might jeopardize and confuse the sense of divine simplicity. The metaphysical positioning of Christ in human hierarchy after the incarnation and his role there is quite a problematic issue as well. The humanity of Christ places him below the ontological reality and perceptibility to divine knowledge even of the lowest angelic rank. What is the role of the incarnated Christ in human hierarchy? Is Christ a bishop? In some sense this might be the case. Christ might be the unique ἀρχή-*bishop*, one of a kind, the divine consecrator of the ecclesiastical hierarchy who ministers in close cooperation with God the Father and the Holy Spirit.[73] Christ, his divinity emphasized, certainly is stated as the source and the teleological goal of every hierarchy.[74] At the same time, the enneadic scheme of the Dionysian metaphysical outlook creates a perfectly harmonious and balanced view, but does not allow for much flexibility in order to preserve and maintain its coherency. This is, perhaps, why our mysterious author, while explicitly referring to Christ's incarnation, still presents Christ's soteriological role in terms of a single divinity working (theurgy) on behalf of human salvation, portrayed in terms not that different from the role that the Thearchy might play through the mediation of angelic orders. What Pseudo-Dionysius states about God in general is applicable to the incarnated Christ only at the expense of his humanhood.[75] The emphasis on the unchanged, unaltered, and essentially transcendent divinity of Christ seems to prevail.[76]

The emphasis on Christ's divinity is dictated not necessarily by Monophysite leanings of the author but by the cosmological perspective of his metaphysical system. Besides, Pseudo-Dionysius openly confesses to be lost on the issue of the incarnation: "The most evident idea in theology, namely, the sacred incarnation of Jesus for our sake, is something which cannot be enclosed in words nor grasped by any mind, not even by the leaders among the front rank of the angels. That he undertook to be a man is, for us, entirely mysterious."[77]

The best Christological solution Pseudo-Dionysius finds is to keep Christological issues in ambiguous tension by quietly withdrawing from their active discussion, while acknowledging key Christian soteriological propositions. Christ in the Dionysian system is God and the Savior who became incarnated. The issues of the economical activity of Christ, such as his death on the Cross and resurrection, are acknowledged. The importance of imitation of Christ, the role of Christ as the example of a properly sinless life, Christ as Educator, his sanctifying activity and power, and participation in and communion with Christ are reflected in the corpus.[78] What is absent is the direct and detailed discussion of the relationship of his human and divine natures, with the enigmatic exception of *Ep.* 4, which in itself does not solve but only illustrates the problem.

Finally, perhaps being sensitive to ongoing Christological debates, the author of the *CD* does not want to state openly his views on the nature of Christ in order to gain a wider readership, which lends more strength to the hypothesis of a literary ploy than to attempted forgery. What is not explicitly stated cannot lead to an open conflict with ongoing Christological controversies. His neutrality or purposeful ambiguity proved to be successful in attracting support for the acceptance of the corpus. It helps to explain why in Late Antiquity most Christologically conflicting groups—Monophysites, Chalcedonians, and even Nestorians—claimed the authority of the corpus as their own. The Dionysian concern was about something else than what divided the camps.

At the same time, regardless of the type of Christianity Pseudo-Dionysius wanted to promote, he considered—and presented—himself to be a Christian.

His adherence to Christianity is only matched with his adherence to Neoplatonism. As troubling as such a union might be for some ancient and modern admirers or critics of the *Areopagitica*, refusal to acknowledge this and find peace with this acknowledgement complicates rather than elucidates Dionysian studies. For instance, Schäfer is correct when he points out that "the key to understanding Dionysius' philosophy is not to interpret him via Proclus, as so many have done for the last hundred years or so and still do."[79] It is also true that we cannot fully appreciate the theology of Pseudo-Dionysius without a thorough study of Proclus and other Neoplatonists, which many have undertaken. As some aspects of the *CD* might not fit perfectly within certain conventional paradigms, especially in Christian traditions where his influence is paramount, the assessment of the Dionysian contribution should not suffer because of some either obscure or dubious elements in the corpus that could make one uncomfortable.

There are several peculiar passages in the text of the corpus that either imply or openly suggest an inclusive approach to acceptance of Greek philosophy. In *Ep.* 6, addressed to some Sosipater, Pseudo-Dionysius writes,

> Do not count it a triumph, reverend Sosipater, that you are denouncing a cult [θρησκείαν] or a point of view which does not seem to be good. And do not imagine that, having thoroughly refuted it, all is therefore well with Sosipater. For it could happen that the one hidden truth could escape both you and others in the midst of falsehoods and appearances. What is not red does not have to be white. What is not a horse is not necessarily a human.[80]

If the rebuke of Sosipater is meant to point to interreligious disputes between Christians and pagans rather than disputes among different Christian camps,[81] this can support the hypothesis about the author's intention to protect what he might consider in Greek philosophy as compatible with Christian teaching. Simply proving that some aspects of Hellenistic learning are wrong does not imply that the *original* source of Greek wisdom is different from the source of Christian revelation. There is only one source of the truth for Pseudo-Dionysius and it is rooted in the One God who benevolently offered it to all nations from the beginning.

In *CH* 9.2–4 (260B–261D) Pseudo-Dionysius defends the view that each nation originally had equal access to the knowledge of God that was revealed to it through a guardian angel. Divine Providence assigned one angel to lead each nation, therefore the number of angels equals the number of nations. Each angel has the same authority and power. The reason why only Jewish people in the Old Testament period were participants in true religion is not because of unfair treatments by Providence, but because the other nations out of their free will went astray from knowledge of the true God and began worshiping idols.[82] The importance of this passage is that it shows that our anonymous author states that the Divine Providence from the beginning treats all peoples equally and that each nation has the same access to divine knowledge communicated through angels if it chooses to follow the revelation given to them. It is not only that there is no preferential treatment in the divine economy, but that each nation in its roots has seeds of the same knowledge of God, which tends to support the positive role of the best of Greek philosophy in leading people to God. If this assumption is correct, here we find an intriguing development in Patristic apologetics. If for Justin and many who followed him, Plato learned and borrowed some aspects of divine truth from Moses, for Pseudo-Dionysius, Moses and Plato *independently* from each other expressed facets of the divine truth. Of course, in the case of Moses divine truth would be more fully expressed, but nevertheless Plato also can be acknowledged for his contributions.

Probably the most revealing passage from the *Areopagitica* where Pseudo-Dionysius explicitly offers his support for Hellenistic wisdom comes from *Ep.* 7. In the same letter he also confesses his familiarity with the "sacred books of the Persians" and the cult of Mithras.[83] In the letter Pseudo-Dionysius presents himself as non-confrontational and, perhaps, a reconciliatory defender of anything that is authentically true whether it comes from scriptural, Hellenistic, or other sources:

> As far as I am concerned I have never spoken out against Greeks or any others. In my view, good men are satisfied to know and to proclaim as well as they can the truth itself as it really is. As soon as anything has been manifested for what is assuredly is by the norm of truth and has been spotlessly established, anything else, anything even with the semblance of truth, will be refuted as alien to and unlike reality, as specious rather than authentic.[84]

Basically, the defense of the truth, as far as our mysterious author sees and understands it, defines the main perspective of the corpus. The contents of the *CD* are an attempt to promulgate this truth, which in his opinion stands for itself.[85] In easily traced biblical, Patristic, and Neoplatonic sources that are intricately interwoven into the fabric of his narrative, one can identify the intention of the author to represent what the author considers to be true in the ultimate sense.

As a concern for the ultimate truth defines the *Areopagitica*, it would be wrong to see our mysterious author as one who blindly endorses any non-Christian source. He gives hints in the text that point to his condemnation of pagan religious perceptions and practices. For example, while praising the virtue of light and the sun, Pseudo-Dionysius clearly rejects "the old myth" that the sun is god and Demiurge of the cosmos.[86] Our anonymous author also is explicit in his criticism of pagan polytheism: the fall of nations from angelic guardianship led them "into the cult of false gods."[87] In order to come to the true knowledge one does not depend on the participation of pagan gods: "No strange gods were in command here [οὐκ ἔκφυλοί τινες ἐπεστάτουν θεοί]."[88] His application of Hellenistic learning is critical and overshadowed by his preference for Christianity. Only truth possessed by Christians is proven "to be more simple and more divine than every other."[89]

VI. The tremendous influence of the *Areopagitica*

An important and well-established fact about the corpus is that it had a significant influence on Christian tradition, both in its Western and Eastern hemispheres. As Campbell observes, "The medieval theologians raised Dionysius to a level far above all the Fathers of the Church, and just a little lower than the inspired writers."[90] To provide the complete and detailed account of the transmission of the *CD* filtered through the centuries after this corpus was written and accepted would require a multivolume publication that would include a list of all major Christian "theologians, mystics, and spiritual writers from the seventh to the sixteenth century."[91] It would not be an exaggeration to go beyond Campbell's estimation and agree with Jaroslav Pelikan that Pseudo-Dionysius experienced an authority that was rivaled only by that of the apostles.[92] The impact of the *Areopagitica* on Christian metaphysics, epistemology, liturgy, mysticism, architecture, sacramentality, hierarchical structuring, and overall spirituality is undeniable. It is hard to imagine how a number of well-established aspects of Christian theology and spirituality might look now if the *CD* would never have been discovered or accepted.

The tremendous influence of the corpus also inadvertently supports the hypothesis of this essay. The pseudonymous attribution proved to be exceptionally effective. Could the actual author of the corpus really envision this success while assigning his writings to Dionysius the Areopagite as their supposed historical author? If this is the case, it would be a rather unbelievably daring and risky enterprise to introduce works under the name of the first-century New Testament character, who, except for the Book of Acts account, where he appears only briefly, and some scarce hagiographical references, was otherwise unknown in Patristic tradition, certainly unknown for his own writings. We do not even have any theological insights or contributions attributed to him that come from oral tradition. Moreover, if we presume the actual author intended to present this corpus as an authentic work of Dionysius, why then undermine himself with poorly designed biographical and historical references (addressed in more detail in the next chapter) that only jeopardize the historical affiliation with the Areopagite rather than solidify it? It is an especially imprudent choice in the fifth and sixth centuries, where the influx of forgeries put everybody on high alert.

To sum up: in spite of the tremendous mystery that surrounds the *CD*, there are several things we know with certainty:

I   Dionysius the Areopagite mentioned in Acts did not write these treatises.
II The integrity of the corpus, both internal and external. What we know as the *Areopagitica* always consisted of the same number closely related works, dated from one period, and written seemingly by one person.
III Regardless of what some scholars might think about the native background of the actual author and the place where he received his education and produced these works, he wrote in Greek.
IV The author of the *CD* was familiar with Neoplatonism to the degree that he can be acknowledged as a Neoplatonic philosopher himself.
V   The author of the *CD* also was well versed in Christian Scriptures and Patristic tradition. He demonstrates authentic knowledge of Christianity and, leaving aside his "denominational" affiliation, can be recognized as a genuine Christian.
VI The tremendous influence that the *Areopagitica* had upon Western and Eastern Christianity cannot be discarded.

All these aspects of the *Areopagitica*, both known ones and the ones that are generally presumed but factually uncertain, are congenial to supporting the hypothesis that attribution of this corpus to Dionysius the Areopagite was a literary ploy. The application of the allonym without an extensive effort to present the works themselves as coming from the first century points rather to a metaphorical role of this first-century apostolic character than an intentional projection of historical falsification. The integrity of the corpus as an interconnected exposition reflecting thematic unity also suggests premeditated literary design, where additionally mentioned titles of otherwise unknown works point to either intended areas for further exploration or issues for which a resolution is already suggested in the extant works of the corpus.

The survival of the *CD* throughout the centuries in the form designed by the author only confirms the appropriateness of its initial indivisible unity and testifies to the author's literary genius. The credit can be shared with John of Scythopolis, assuming he is not the author, but the first known editor who was responsible for a *critical* edition of the *Areopagitica*, from which all existing Greek manuscripts originate.[93]

Incorporation of Neoplatonic and Patristic materials in creatively developed discourse might point to a desire to find a suitable response that can adequately express what it means to be a civilized Roman-Byzantine Christian, where the cultural standards of Hellenistic antiquity find, or at least are looking for, a homogeneous agreement with Christian tradition. This at times unhappy and mutually confrontational interaction between Hellenistic culture and Christianity is a common feature of imperial Christianity for centuries, including Christian communities on Roman territories before the legalization of Christianity. There was a search for conclusive resolution. Any effort to formulate issues related to Roman-Greek civilized identity could only be expressed in the Greek, not Syrian, language. Greek was the leading medium of all major philosophical and theological discourse at the time. The tremendous influence of the corpus is the major indicator that its content hit the right target.

There is no doubt that the assumed identity of the author of the corpus produced unprecedented outcomes. Whether this was the intentional premeditation of the author or an unexpected consequence remains a mystery. Apart from the indisputable fact that Dionysius the Areopagite of the first century did not write the body of works assigned to his name and that the original version of the *CD* was written in Greek, some of the aspects and issues discussed, upon closer look, appear to be not so definite indicators of the historical background of the *Areopagitica* in relation to the issue of authorship. At least, they are not so conclusive about the actual intentions of the author. They are rather indicative of the scholarly attitudes of particular students of Pseudo-Dionysius, who either want to present the corpus as exclusively Neoplatonic or authentically Christian. They, nevertheless, are helpful in providing additional support for the hypothesis stated in this monograph. A closer look at what the text of the corpus states about the identity of its author and how seriously it attempts to portray the first-century milieu may lead to conclusions that are not so straightforward as generally are assumed.

Notes

1 See, for example, Emmanuel Bulhak, *Authenticité des oeuvres de saint Denys l'Aréopagite,* évêque *d'Athènes et de Lutetia in Parisiis et sa réintégration sur la siège épiscopal de Paris* (Rome, 1938).
2 Arthur, *Pseudo-Dionysius as Polemicist,* 144–45.
3 With the minor exception of *Ep.* 11 (PG 3:1120–22) that was viewed as spurious a long time before Koch and Stiglmayr. See Copp, *Dionysius the*

42 Conventionally accepted facets of the CD

Pseudo-Areopagite, 145–46. Copp suggests that Hilduin, the ninth-century abbot of the Abbey of St. Denys, might be a possible candidate for an author of Ep. 11.
4 Hathaway, Hierarchy and the Definition of Order, 61. See also Rorem, Pseudo-Dionysius: A Commentary, 3–46; Golitzin, "Dionysius Areopagita: A Christian Mysticism?" 169–71; Schäfer, Philosophy of Dionysius the Areopagite, 11, etc.
5 With few minor recent exceptions. See, for example, Bernard Brons, "Sekundäre Textparteien im Corpus Pseudo-Dionysiacum? Literarkritische Beobachtungen zu ausgewählten Textstellen," Nachrichten der Akademie der Wissenschaften in Göttingen: Philologisch-Historisch Klasse 5 (1975): 99–140; Mihai Nasta, "Quatre Etats de la Textualité dans l'Histoire du Corpus Dionyseinne," in Denys l'Aréopagite et sa Posterité en Orient et en Occident, ed. Ysabel de Andia (Paris: Institut d'Études Augustiniennes, 1997), 31–65.
6 In DN on several occasions The Symbolic Theology is referred to as not written yet, see DN 1.8 (597B), 4.5 (700C), 9.5 (913B), 13.4 (984A). In CH 15.6 (336A) our anonymous author mentions The Symbolic Theology as an already finished work and in MT 3 (1033AB) and Ep. 9.6 (1113BC) he provides a summary of the treatise. Ep. 9.1 (1104B) also indicates that this treatise was addressed to Timothy. The length and content of Ep. 9 led some scholars to assume that this letter could be the treatise itself, "but the inconsistencies of this have proved too difficult" (Hathaway, Hierarchy and the Definition of Order, 67).
7 DN 1.1 (585B), 2.3 (640B), 2.7 (645A), 11.5 (953B); in DN 1.5 (593B), 2.1 (636C-637A) and MT 3 (1032D-1033A) Pseudo-Dionysius provides a summary remarks about the treatise. The Theological Representations was addressed also to Timothy, DN 1.1 (585B).
8 DN 4.2 (696B). This treatise could be identical with The Celestial Hierarchy.
9 DN 4.2 (696C).
10 DN 4.35 (736B).
11 CH 7.4 (212B).
12 EH 1.2 (373B), 2.3.2 (397C).
13 Louth, Denys the Areopagite, 20; idem, "The Reception of Dionysius up to Maximus the Confessor," in Re-Thinking Dionysius the Areopagite, 49. Cf. René Roques, L'univers dionysien: Structure hiérarchique du monde selon le Pseudo-Denys (Paris: Aubier, 1954), 128–33; idem, "Denys l'Aréopagite (Le Pseudo-)," in Dictionnaire de spiritualité ascétique et mystique, eds. Édouard des Places, Irénée H. Dalmais, and Gustave Bardy (Paris: Beauchesne, 1957), 3:259–62.
14 Balthasar, "Denys," 2:154–64.
15 Cf. Franz Mali, "Hat die Schrift 'De symbolica theologia' von Dionysius Ps.-Areopagita gegeben? Anmerkungen zu den Nachrichten des Sergius von Rēš'ainā über Dionysius Ps.-Areopagita," in Syriaca: Zur Geschichte, Theologie, Liturgie und Gegenwartslage der syrischen Kirche 2: Deutsches Syrologen-Symposium (Juli 2000, Wittenberg), ed. Martin Tamcke (Hamburg: Lit, 2002), 213–24.
16 Perczel, "The Earliest Syriac Reception of Dionysius," 31.
17 Perczel, "The Earliest Syriac Reception of Dionysius," 31.
18 Stang, Apophasis and Pseudonymity in Dionysius the Areopagite, 26.
19 His candidacy as the author of the CD was proposed by Irénée Hausherr, "Doutes au sujet du 'Divin Denys'," Orientalia Christiana Periodica 2 (1936): 489; and Balthasar, "Das Scholienwerk des Johannes von Scythopolis," Scholastik 15

(1940): 38; English translation by Brian Daley, Balthasar, "The Problem of the Scholia to Pseudo-Dionysius," in *Cosmic Liturgy: The Universe According to Maximus the Confessor* (San Francisco, CA: Ignatius Press, 2003), 385. Cf. Roques, "Denys l'Aréopagite (le Pseudo-)," 3:255. Recently his authorship was advocated by Arthur, *Pseudo-Dionysius as Polemicist*, 138, 184–87, 197.
20 *PG* 29:507–8.
21 Albert Jahn, *Eclogae e Proclo de Philosophia Chaldaica; sive de doctrina oraculorum Chaldaicorum* (Halle: Pfeffer, 1891), 62–64.
22 Martin Sicherl, "Ein Neuplatonischer Hymnus unter den Gedichten Gregors von Nazianz," in *Gonimos: Neoplatonic and Byzantine Studies Presented to Leendert G. Westerink at 75*, eds. J. Duffy and J. Peradotto (Buffalo, NJ: Arethusa, 1988), 61–83.
23 Henri-Dominique Saffrey, *Proclus: hymnes et prières* (Paris: Arfuyen, 1994), 75, 78–79.
24 Perczel, "Denys l'Aréopagite, lecteur d'Origène," in *Origeniana Séptima: Orígenes in den Auseinandersetzungen des 4. Jahrhunderts*, eds. W. A. Bienert and U. Kühneweg (Leuven: Leuven University Press and Uitgeverij Peeters, 1999), 673–710, esp. 690–702; idem, "The Pseudo-Didymian 'De trinitate' and Pseudo-Dionysius the Areopagite: A Preliminary Study," *Studia Patristica* 58 (2013): 83–108.
25 Bernard McGinn, *The Foundations of Mysticism: Origins to the Fifth Century* (New York, NY: Crossroad Publishing, 1995), 163.
26 See Hathaway, *Hierarchy and the Definition of Order*; Rorem, *Pseudo-Dionysius: A Commentary*; Golitzin, "Dionysius Areopagita: A Christian Mysticism?" 170–80 with emphasis on *Ep*. 10. However, if Golitzin finds in the letters the password for Christian understanding of the entire corpus, Hathaway finds there certainly a Neoplatonic one.
27 Rorem, *Pseudo-Dionysius: A Commentary*, 18.
28 Stiglmayr, "Der sogenannte Dionysius Areopagita und Severus von Antiochien," 1–27, 161–89; idem, "Um eine Ehrenrettung des Severus von Antiochen," 52–67.
29 For extensive treatment of Syrian influences see especially Golitzin, *Et Introibo Ad Altare Dei*, 354–92; cf. idem, *Mystagogy*, 324–63.
30 Golitzin, "Dionysius Areopagita: A Christian Mysticism?" 163n5.
31 Golitzin, *Mystagogy*, 363.
32 This approach was proposed by Endre von Ivánka, "La Signification historique du 'Corpus Areopagiticum'," *Recherches de Science Religieuse* 36 (1949): 5–24; idem, *Plato Christianus: Übernahme und Umgestaltung des Platonismus durch die Väter* (Einsiedeln: Johannes Verlag, 1964).
33 Golitzin, "Dionysius Areopagita: A Christian Mysticism?" 180.
34 Golitzin, *Mystagogy*, 324–29.
35 Golitzin, *Et Introibo Ad Altare Dei*, 43; cf. idem, *Mystagogy*, XXXVII.
36 Golitzin, *Et Introibo Ad Altare Dei*, 233–354 and 354–92 respectively.
37 See ch 1, endnote 10, p. 18.
38 Louth, *Denys the Areopagite*, 81.
39 Cf. Arthur, *Pseudo-Dionysius as Polemicist*, 157–59.
40 *EH* 1.1 (369A-372A).
41 *EH* 1.5 (377A); PTS 36:68; Pseudo-Dionysius, *The Complete Works* (New York, NY: Paulist Press, 1987), 199–200. Cf. *CH* 2.5 (145C), *DN* 1.8 (597C), and *MT* 1.2 (1000A).

42 Eusebius of Caesarea, *EH* 3.4.
43 Angelo Di Berardino, ed., *Patrology: The Eastern Fathers from the Council of Chalcedon (451) to John of Damascus (†750)* (Cambridge, UK: James Clarke & Co, 2006), 359–60.
44 *Ep.* 8 might indicate this.
45 Louth, *Denys the Areopagite*, 68–69. Cf. *DN* 6.1.3 (532D—533A), 6.3.2 (533D—536A).
46 Compare, for example, Louth, *Denys the Areopagite*, 70; and Golitzin, "Dionysius Areopagita: A Christian Mysticism?" 174–78.
47 Adolf Harnack, *History of Dogma* (Eugene, OR: Wipf and Stock, 1997), 3:155.
48 Golitzin, *Et Introibo Ad Altare Dei*, 22.
49 Arthur, *Pseudo-Dionysius as Polemicist*, 13–19, 58–69, 101–39.
50 Arthur, *Pseudo-Dionysius as Polemicist*, 58–69.
51 Arthur, *Pseudo-Dionysius as Polemicist*, 65.
52 There is a well-established Neoplatonic tradition that comes from Syria. Iamblichus most likely was born there and later held his school in the Syrian city of Apamea (Clarke, Dillon, and Hershbell, *Iamblichus: De Mysteriis*, XXII-XXIII; see also Eunapius, *VS*, LCL 134:362–77). "A Syriac-speaking city on the boarder of Byzantium and Persia, Harran had enjoyed a measure of religious tolerance the Byzantine authorities denied to cities that were more fully under Christian military control. Upon the closure of the Platonic Academy in Athens in 529, its leading lights, Damascius and Simplicius, had fled to Persia, only to return three years later to Syria. In Harran, Damascius appears to have founded a Platonic School, in the uninterrupted Iamblichian tradition, that remained a going concern as late as the 10th century, when a Muslim traveller visited and described the school building" (Daniel Merkur, "Reflections on the Meaning of Theosophy," *Theosophical History* 7 (1998): 20; Polymnia Athanassiadi, "Persecution and Response in Late Paganism: The Evidence of Damascius," *The Journal of Hellenic Studies* 113 (1993): 25–27).
53 Richard T. Wallis, *Neoplatonism*, 2nd ed. (Indianapolis, IN: Hackett Publishing Company, 1995), 141.
54 *Or.* 43.14; SC 384:146–48; FC 22:38.
55 Eunapius, *VS*, LCL 134:512–13.
56 Eunapius, *VS*, LCL 134:514–15.
57 See also Hathaway, *Hierarchy and the Definition of Order*, 19–21.
58 Athanassiadi, "Persecution and Response in Late Paganism," 23; cf. idem, "Introduction," in Damascius, *The Philosophical History*, trans. Polymnia Athanassiadi (Athens, Greece: Apamea, 1999), 46–47, 343–47.
59 Sara Ahbel-Rappe, "Introduction to the Life and Philosophy of Damascius," in Damascius, *Problems and Solutions Concerning First Principles*, trans. Sara Ahbel-Rappe (Oxford: Oxford University Press, 2010), 4.
60 Arthur, *Pseudo-Dionysius as Polemicist*, 144, 171.
61 Thomas Campbell, "Introduction," in Dionysius the Pseudo-Areopagite, *The Ecclesiastical Hierarchy*, trans. Thomas L. Campbell (Washington, DC: University Press of America, 1981), 11–12, 100–1.
62 Cf. Wear and Dillon, *Dionysius the Areopagite and the Neoplatonist Tradition*, 11–13.
63 The initial identification of Peter the Iberian as possible author of the *CD* was proposed by Ernst Honigmann, *Pierre l'Ibérien et les écrits du pseudo Denys l'Aréopagite* (Brussels: Académie Royale de Belgique, 1952), later reexamined

Conventionally accepted facets of the CD   45

by Esbroeck, "Peter the Iberian and Dionysius the Areopagite: Honigmann's Thesis Revisited," 217–27.
64 Golitzin, *Mystagogy*, 399–406, cf. idem, *Et Introibo Ad Altare Dei*, 415–21.
65 See Cornelia J. de Vogel, "Platonism and Christianity: A Mere Antagonism or a Profound Common Ground?" *Vigiliae Christianae* 39 (1985): 1–62.
66 Eric Perl, *Theophany: The Neoplatonic Philosophy of Dionysius the Areopagite* (Albany, NY: State University of New York Press, 2007). See also Wear and Dillon, *Dionysius the Areopagite and the Neoplatonist Tradition*; Schäfer, *Philosophy of Dionysius the Areopagite*; and Stephen Gersh, *From Iamblichus to Eriugena: An Investigation of the Prehistory and Evolution of the Pseudo-Dionysian Tradition* (Leiden: Brill, 1978).
67 Wear and Dillon, *Dionysius the Areopagite and the Neoplatonist Tradition*, 11.
68 Gersh, *From Iamblichus to Eriugena*, 4. Cf. Alexandre Kojève, *Essai d'une histoire raisonnée de la philosophie païenne III* (Paris: Gallimard, 1973), 474n59.
69 This one seems to be of the most persistent attributions. See Hathaway, *Hierarchy and the Definition of Order*, 17–19, 25–29; Rosemary Griffith, "Neo-Platonism and Christianity: Pseudo-Dionysius and Damascius," *Studia Patristica* 29 (1997): 238–43; Carlo Maria Mazzucchi, "Damascio, autore del 'Corpus Dionysiacum', e il dialogo Περὶ πολιτικῆς ἐπιστήμης," *Aevum* 80 (2006): 299–334; and Lankila, "The 'Corpus Areopagiticum' as a Crypto-Pagan Project," 14–40. Cf. Golitzin, *Mystagogy*, XXVIII–XXXI.
70 Louth, "The Reception of Dionysius up to Maximus the Confessor," 50.
71 Super-transcendence in this case indicates not only that the essence of God beyond human comprehension, but also that God as the cause of any essence transcends any notion of essence and existence in himself. The true realm of the Thearchy for Pseudo-Dionysius is existence as non-existence and the ontological status of God as non-being. For the Thearchy to be the source and cause of any existents to come into existence indicates that existence and being cannot be applied to God. Otherwise the caused and the Cause would interrelate and belong to the same metaphysical realm and, as such, have to derive their existence from something that is above them.
72 Arguably, *The Human Hierarchy* might be a more fitting title for the *EH* as a more accurate description of what the actual content of the corpus might have intended (see, Pseudo-Dionysius, *The Complete Works*, 195n2).
73 *EH* 5.3.5 (512C).
74 *EH* 1.2 (373B); 5.1.5 (505B).
75 See *CH* 4.4, 7.2 (208C); *EH* 1.1 (372AB), 3.3.13 (444CD); 4.3.10 (484A); *DN* 1.4 (592AB).
76 *Ep.* 3–4, 8.1 (1085CD).
77 *DN* 2.9 (648A); PTS 33:133; Pseudo-Dionysius, *The Complete Works*, 65.
78 See *EH* 2.3.6 (401D), 3.3.12 (444AB), 5.3.4 (512AB), 7.1.2 (553C); *DN* 11.5 (953AB).
79 Schäfer, *Philosophy of Dionysius the Areopagite*, 163.
80 *Ep.* 6 (1077A); PTS 36:164; Pseudo-Dionysius, *The Complete Works*, 266.
81 The key word is θρησκεία-"cult," "religion" (*Ep.* 6 [1077A]) that in this context might be more indicative of a particular religious tradition than of denominational disagreements within one particular religious tradition.
82 Cf. *Ep.* 7.2 (1080B).
83 *Ep.* 7.2 (1081A); PTS 36:168; Pseudo-Dionysius, *The Complete Works*, 268.
84 *Ep.* 7.1 (1077BC); PTS 36:165; Pseudo-Dionysius, *The Complete Works*, 266.

46 *Conventionally accepted facets of the* CD

85 *Ep.* 7.1 (1080A).
86 *DN* 4.4 (700C). Cf. *DN* 11.6 (953D).
87 *CH* 9.3 (260C); PTS 36:37; Pseudo-Dionysius, *The Complete Works*, 171.
88 *CH* 9.3 (261A); PTS 36:38; Pseudo-Dionysius, *The Complete Works*, 172.
89 *DN* 7.4 (873A); PTS 33:199–200; Pseudo-Dionysius, *The Complete Works*, 110.
90 Campbell, "Introduction," in Dionysius the Pseudo-Areopagite, *The Ecclesiastical Hierarchy*, 14.
91 Campbell, "Introduction," in Dionysius the Pseudo-Areopagite, *The Ecclesiastical Hierarchy*, 12. For overviews of influence, see André Rayez, "Denys l'Aréopagite (Le Pseudo-): IV, Influence du Pseudo-Denys en Orient," in *Dictionnaire de spiritualité ascétique et mystique*, 3:286–318; Various Authors, "Denys l'Aréopagite (Le Pseudo-): V, Influence du Pseudo-Denys en Occident," in *Dictionnaire de spiritualité ascétique et mystique*, 3:318–429; Rorem, *Pseudo-Dionysius: A Commentary*, 29–46, 73–90, 118–32, 167–81, 214–40.
92 Jaroslav Pelikan, "Introduction," in Pseudo-Dionysius, *The Complete Works*, 21.
93 See Beate Regina Suchla, ed., *Corpus Dionysiacum I: De Divinis Nominibus*, PTS 33 (New York, NY: Walter de Gruyter, 1990), 36–64; idem, "Die Überlieferung des Prologs des Johannes von Skythopolis," 4:176–88; idem, "Eine Redaktion des grieshischen Corpus Dionysiacum Areopagiticum im Umkreis des Johannes von Skythopolis: Ein dritter Beitrag zur Überlieferungsgeschichte des CD," *Nachrichten der Akademie der Wissenschaften in Göttingen: Philologisch-Historische Klasse* 4 (1985): 177–93; idem, *Dionysius Areopagita*, 62–63.

3 How serious was the author of the *CD* about the first-century environment?

Christopher Beeley correctly points out the major shift that occurred in the fifth century. In the fourth century Patristic authors made direct and indirect references to earlier authorities, especially Origen, while their main presumption remained that they were under the essential authority of the Scriptures. In the perception of fifth-century Christians, such fathers as Athanasius of Alexandria and the Cappadocians became authoritative sources of orthodoxy in their own right, along with the Scriptures.[1] It was the time of the birth of authoritative and also personified Church tradition. It was not without contribution to this development from such fathers as Basil of Caesarea, where the meaning of truthfulness of Christian orthodoxy became associated not only with the Scriptures and with somewhat general and to some degree geographically specific understanding of Christian rule of faith as its supplement but also with the Scriptures and personal representatives or witnesses to the rule of faith. The orthodoxy of the Christian Church became the Christianity of Athanasius or Gregory of Nazianzus, or Christianity in the spirit of Athanasius or Gregory of Nazianzus.

This perception of personal authoritative fathers as pillars and defenders of orthodoxy inadvertently contributed to and encouraged extensive pseudonymous literary activity, which became prominent during that time (as well as afterwards). Numerous anonymous works began circulating under the names of universally upheld authorities in order to secure the intended by anonymous authors form of orthodoxy. It helped to promote ideas that seemed to be important to anonymous authors without regard to how these ideas correlate with the actual views of the fathers who were declared to be the authors of these counterfeited works. Other common reasons to write under pseudonyms in the Patristic period might be dictated by concerns for personal safety, such as fear of persecution, exile, or charges of heresy, especially in such turbulent times as the fifth and sixth centuries. Assigning a work to an accepted authority usually helped to secure both its survival and a wider readership.

In this case, the mysterious author of the *CD*, or perhaps his first enthusiastic readers, were clever to attract wide readership by assigning Dionysius as the author. Who would not want to read works from the apostolic period that were not heard of before? Name recognition, even in the form of an endorsement, still helps to sell books or other valuables. If this is the case, the *Areopagitica* would be in line with a common practice that encouraged a proliferation of forgeries. If it could be shown that works belonged to the authorship of someone who was accepted as a saint of the past—and Dionysius the Areopagite certainly fit the profile—this acceptance also, somewhat automatically, testified to the orthodoxy of the writings.

For the same reason, however, and on the same grounds, assigning Dionysius as the author would jeopardize the acceptance of the corpus as authentic. Attribution of writings to any New Testament figure in itself seems to have been a dangerous enterprise, for it could be easily established as a forgery, especially that late in history, but the selection of an author who otherwise was not attested in the Patristic tradition was even more disadvantageous. Dionysius the Areopagite is known in Christian tradition for his sainthood, but not for his orthodox—or in this case *any*—writings. Selecting him as the author only contributes to a straightforward discovery of the forgery rather than helping to conceal it. Would it make more sense to forge as an author one of the established authorities, like Athanasius, or the Cappadocian Fathers, or Cyril of Alexandria? All of them experienced *incredible popularity* as covers for pseudonymous authors.

Deliberately choosing Dionysius of the first century as the author is quite a risky plan if the actual author wanted to present the corpus as an original production. What also is interesting is that our mysterious author does not seem to work hard in promulgating the Dionysian authorship. This attribution is not as explicitly stated in the text of the corpus, despite centuries-long acceptance of Dionysius the Areopagite as author. One often overlooked fact is that a scrutiny of the text of the corpus does not reveal much personal information about either the actual or the alleged author. There is a sense that identification of the *CD* with Dionysius the Areopagite was not the main objective of the actual author. Even though the association of the *CD* with the name of Dionysius the Areopagite was introduced simultaneously with the first recorded appearance of the corpus in the early sixth century, apart from introductory prefaces where we encounter such verbalizations as "Dionysius the Elder to Timothy the Fellow-Elder," which in their turn could be the work of a later editorial process,[2] the author of the corpus refers to himself by the name of Dionysius (however, without title "the Areopagite") only once in *Ep.* 7.3 (1081C). Even in this instance the explicit use of the name Dionysius should be looked at more closely. The authenticity of this letter certainly could be questioned, if not in its entirety, then at least in part. Some parts of it could be written by someone other than the actual author of the *CD*.[3]

With regard to the name Dionysius there is another possibility: that the *CD* was written by somebody with the name Dionysius—a name not uncommon in Late Antiquity—as either his personal reflections or in response to some inquiries of his friends, and only later became associated with the better known Dionysius of the first century. In this case we might be dealing not with Pseudo-Dionysius the Areopagite, but with Dionysius the Pseudo-Areopagite.

Perhaps the author of the corpus was a woman. There are several well-educated and learned Byzantine empresses who, usually through the stylus of their husbands, were involved in the theological affairs of the church. Sometimes clever empresses, without bothering with writing, through the political power their husbands' imperial purple, were able to exercise direct influence in theological matters. What would an educated woman not married to the emperor do? She could write under the assumed name of a *male* saint, since female saints of Patristic times were not much known for their own writings. To get a real attention it should be the voice of either the Mother of God herself (a really daring prospect) or, more modestly, some saintly male. The effect is magnified if this male is from the apostolic circle. The weight of apostolicity combined with no restrictions in the style of writing (as there is no need to imitate the writing patterns of any known authorities) were certainly attractive factors that could inspire any woman to communicate her ideas undetectably. Frankly, it is possible but not likely. If a woman would write on this subject it might have a more picturesque and interesting approach, and a more passionate style. Her work certainly would not sound like a work on the *theory* of mysticism, but would speak out of personal experience. A female author, perhaps, would be less interested in building predominantly male hierarchies and attempting to squeeze the whole universe into a coherent system. Nevertheless, can anybody imagine—if Augustine was a black African and Pseudo-Dionysius was a woman, then there would not be much that is white or male in the foundation of our Western white male patriarchal civilization. However, to continue this line of inquiry will transform this discourse into the genre of pure theological fiction. The bottom line is that we do not know from the text or other external sources what precisely inspired the assignment of these works to Dionysius the Areopagite. We also do not know whether it was a deliberate choice of the author or a successful and masterfully managed attribution by his first enthusiastic readers.

Such supporters of the authenticity of the *CD* in Late Antiquity as John of Scythopolis, who is also responsible for a *critical* edition of the *CD* from which all existing Greek manuscripts originate, certainly contributed to the reinforcement of the connection between this corpus and the historical Dionysius the Areopagite. Attempts to win the acceptance of the *Areopagitica* took seriously both historicity and orthodoxy, which worked in a kind of paradoxical reverse. They attempted to prove historicity through defense of orthodoxy by the way of explaining troubling passages in an orthodox sense, and then from historicity (including scant historical references to people and events scattered throughout the *CD* taken uncritically) to explain other troubling, especially Proclian, passages. This becomes already apparent in the first *Scholia* on the corpus written by John of Scythopolis.

Textual evidence, however, does not reveal much personal information about the author, including his assumed pseudepigraphic identity. It indicates that the author did not wish to insist on the Areopagite identity to the degree that subsequent acceptance of the corpus required. He certainly did not want to reveal his identity, or, if we are dealing with private correspondence among a small circle of intellectuals, he did not have to. For example, Perczel inclines "to believe that the original CD was never meant to be widely read but was instead produced for a select, esoteric audience of Origenists."[4] Pseudonymity in this context was a kind of protection from censorship. It was only the later work of Greek commentators, such as John of Scythopolis, that, according to Perczel, adapted the *Areopagitica* to a wider esoteric and mainstream readership.

Balthasar suggests that the actual author simply transferred to the apostolic period his personal, theological, and spiritual relationships, and basically codified his friends and opponents.[5] Balthasar additionally hints that further research into the circle of the first supporters of the *Areopagitica*, such as John of Scythopolis or Sergius of Reshaina, might reveal among them the actual author of the corpus.[6] If John of Scythopolis, whom Balthasar calls "the great 'Christianizer' of Pseudo-Dionysius,"[7] is the actual author of the corpus, it certainly would be ingenious, but quite dishonest, on his part to write the *Areopagitica* and then a commentary on his own works to secure their acceptance.[8] Saffrey and Golitzin believe that John of Scythopolis, if not an author, at least knew the identity of the author.[9]

In addition to John of Scythopolis and Sergius of Reshaina, John Philoponus and Severus of Antioch might have known the identity of the author or, at least, known of him.[10] Recently, Rosemary Arthur revisited the hypothesis of Sergius of Reshaina as the author of the corpus.[11] Hathaway, who agrees that Sergius comes close to being the author of the corpus but does not think it is the case, quotes Sergius's remark about the reason for Dionysian pseudonymity,

> Everything that one is not permitted to say, and *that which a man is prohibited from speaking about with elevation, in marveling manner, and in public*, he has consigned to his [Dionysius's] holy books, because there he might speak divinely [i.e., with the conventional obscurity].[12]

Here, again, if Sergius of Reshaina is not the author he might have some kind of close personal connection with the actual author, not to mention that Sergius was the first translator of the *CD* into Syriac. Wear and Dillon suggest that the author of the *CD* might belong to the circle of Severus of Antioch and might have been known by him.[13]

On the other hand, if this is the case and John of Scythopolis, John Philoponus, Severus of Antioch, and Sergius of Reshaina knew the actual author, their insistence on connection of this body of writings with a first-century figure, which John of Scythopolis, John Philoponus, and Sergius of Reshaina clearly did (Severus of Antioch only cited the *CD*), only makes them complicit in promulgating a forgery, which does not depict them in likable light. They were among the first supporters of the authenticity of the corpus—the first enthusiastic readers. In some sense it is possible to give them some benefit of the doubt. They actually might believe that the *Areopagitica* was a first-century work. In either case, the overall conclusion that could be drawn from reading the *CD* in the search for its author's conscious attempts to present his writings as coming from the first century is that he does not work very hard to masquerade his writings as such. He does not quote or refer to Paul or any other biblical and Patristic sources just to mask his Neoplatonic inclinations either. In the context of his unmasked, often verbatim, borrowings from Proclus and other non-Christian Neoplatonic sources, Pseudo-Dionysius was often accused of a lack of ingenuity and imagination, and viewed as an unsophisticated compiler who did not do a thorough job in his forgery.

Leaving aside the issue of his ingenuity, which could be a matter of personal preference,[14] his open borrowings from Neoplatonic, Patristic, and biblical sources seem to reflect his free, creative, and learned process of writing unrestricted from any boundaries that could curb a fifth- or sixth-century author posing as the first-century Areopagite. Pseudo-Dionysius uses his sources generously and openly according to literary conventions of the time, not purposefully trying to disguise them. Moreover, he cites Christian sources together with Neoplatonic ones as mutually beneficial and as corresponding with the truth; at least in the form he might have understood it. He does not hide his Neoplatonic sympathies or his Christianity. If Pseudo-Dionysius really wanted to hide his Neoplatonism and portray the first-century Christian environment, he easily could have done a better job. He can be evasive when he wants to be.[15]

In spite of the scant evidence that suggests any conscious desire of the author to portray his writings as coming from the first century, Dionysius the Areopagite, nevertheless, is the assigned author. The main reason for justification of such selection might lie in the sophisticated and creative approach to the authority of major Patristic authors that was happening at the time, in conjunction with certain literary designs proposed in this monograph. It is simply a literary design that took in consideration the emerging role of Patristic authorities as personified representatives for Christian orthodoxy. By using the known name of a saint from the apostolic period, orthodoxy is acknowledged and reassured, but this acknowledgement has more literary contextualization in the content of the corpus than points of historical affiliation. Therefore, the fact that nothing is known about theological specifics of the first-century Dionysius is not important. Apostolic connection and Patristic authority were projected not in historical perspective, but in metaphorical one. This literary approach effectively reflects the fifth- and sixth-century appeal to the authority of individual fathers as preservers of orthodoxy where the figure of the authoritative father has symbolic implications. It is possible to arrive at a similar conclusion if we assess the role of the so-called Dionysian society.

Notes

1 Christopher A. Beeley, *The Unity of Christ: Continuity and Conflict in Patristic Tradition* (New Haven, CT: Yale University Press, 2012), 256–57.
2 Pseudo-Dionysius, *The Complete Works*, 49n2. Their inauthenticity was already asserted in the sixth century, see John of Scythopolis, *SchCH*; PG 4:85C.
3 See Brons, "Sekundäre Textparteien im Corpus Pseudo-Dionysiacum?" 5:99–140; Kharlamov, *The Beauty of the Unity and the Harmony of the Whole*, 81–82.
4 Perczel, "The Earliest Syriac Reception of Dionysius," 35.
5 Balthasar, "Denys," 2:150–51.
6 See Balthasar, "The Problem of the Scholia to Pseudo-Dionysius," 385. Originally published as Balthasar, "Das Scholienwerk des Johannes von Skythopolis," 16–39, of interest p. 38.
7 Balthasar, "The Problem of the Scholia to Pseudo-Dionysius," 381.
8 Cf. Hausherr, "Doutes au sujet de 'divin Denys,'" 484–90.
9 Henri-Dominique Saffrey, "Un lien objectif entre le Pseudo-Denys et Proclus," *Studia Patristica* 9 (1966): 98–105; Golitzin, *Et Introibo Ad Altare Dei*, 345.
10 Golitzin, *Mystagogy*, 405.
11 Arthur, *Pseudo-Dionysius as Polemicist*, 116–21, 138, 184–87, 197.

12 Sergius of Reshaina, and Polycarp Sherwood, "Mimro de Serge de Resayna sur la vie spirituelle," *L'Orient Syrien* 6 (1961): 149. Cit. in Hathaway, *Hierarchy and the Definition of Order*, 25 (emphasis and brackets are in Hathaway).
13 Wear and Dillon, *Dionysius the Areopagite and the Neoplatonist Tradition*, 3–4.
14 Even though it should be acknowledged that some aspects of the *CD* do leave a sense of an artificially constructed, mechanical presentation designed to fit an already predetermined pattern or scheme. The main influence behind his metaphysical vision is Neoplatonic philosophy. The works of Proclus and Damascius, for that matter, share a similar sense of schematism and artificiality, and stand in striking contrast to the more charismatic and visionary philosophy of Plotinus.
15 Cf. Copp, *Dionysius the Pseudo-Areopagite*, 256.

4 The Dionysian society

If the author of the corpus does not refer to himself by name, except for one instance and in prefaces, there are a number of other names mentioned in the *CD*, sometimes as addressees, that have been interpreted as our mysterious author's attempt to project a first-century apostolic and sub-apostolic milieu. We find references to Timothy,[1] Titus,[2] the apostle John,[3] the apostle Peter,[4] James "the brother of God,"[5] Justus,[6] Sosipater,[7] Gaius,[8] Bartholomew (presumably the apostle),[9] Hierotheus,[10] Bishop Polycarp (presumably of Smyrna),[11] Clement the Philosopher (presumably of Rome, according to John of Scythopolis, or the Clement mentioned by Paul in Phil. 4:3),[12] Ignatius (presumably of Antioch),[13] Carpus,[14] Doropheus,[15] Elymas the Magician,[16] Demophilus,[17] Apollophanes,[18] and mad Simon.[19] Some of them are easily recognized, some are only briefly mentioned in the New Testament, some belong to the Apostolic Fathers, some seem to belong to later times, and some are totally unknown.

In assessing the Dionysian society it is difficult to see how this extensive and seemingly random rather than well-thought-out collage of names helps in projecting the first-century environment. It serves more to jeopardize a historical situating of the corpus than to establish it, assuming that the actual author intentionally wanted to present the corpus as a first-century document. However, if viewed from the perspective of the proposed hypothesis of this book, there is important literary significance in how this society functions in the corpus that helps to convey the elevated positioning of Dionysius within it. This metaphorical significance is advantageous for the overall impression that the *Areopagitica* imposes on the reader and it is done in such a sophisticated and tactful way that the elevated positioning of Dionysius in the corpus has not the person but the content of his message in focus.

As has already been discussed,[20] the metaphorical significance of assigning the corpus to Dionysius the Areopagite as a clever *marketing* trick to attract a greater readership presented the external application of the author's literary ploy. The internal application of this literary design is closely interwoven with the role of Dionysian society, and it is even more revealing.

If the so-called Dionysian society in the *Areopagitica* is taken seriously, it is possible to arrive at an impression of a rather elevated status of Dionysius within it. He is intricately portrayed not simply as one of the Apostolic Fathers but as one on almost an equal footing with other apostles, sometimes at the expense of the authority of Paul. Dionysius is portrayed in the corpus as the intimate friend of apostles who followed Christ in his earthly ministry: John, Peter, Bartholomew, and also the brother of Jesus, James. In other words, it places Dionysius in immediate proximity to the apostles handpicked by Christ himself, and his friendship with them consequently helps to add significance to his own status, whereas Paul, who is not among the twelve founding pillars of Christianity, often finds himself in polemical tension with either the church in Jerusalem or with the apostle Peter, rather than in idyllic harmony with them.

If we accept the traditional view of the gathering of apostles with other New Testament notables at the Dormition of Mary,[21] it would make Dionysius the close friend of the Mother of God, too—a thing Paul never claimed for himself. Furthermore, surprisingly, Dionysius never speaks about the effect and experience of being converted to Christianity by Paul. There is no unambiguous reference in the *Areopagitica* to Paul as one who converted our author to Christianity. His conversion to Christianity by Paul is more presupposed than explicitly stated, while the description of the solar eclipse at the time of Christ's crucifixion[22] already suggests that even before he met Paul at Athens he was what Karl Rahner would call an "anonymous Christian," by virtue of witnessing Christ's death and comprehending the true meaning of the eclipse. In a way, the Christianity of Dionysius predates the Christianity of Paul and places him in immediate connection with the historical Christ. Paul only finished the process of his Christian initiation.

The authority of Paul might be seen as minimized in several more instances. For example, Dionysius addresses Timothy in a patronizing demeanor as a father superior to his spiritual son,[23] not only in the manner typical of Paul in his letters to Timothy, but with an even stronger sense of spiritual superiority. Dionysius in his presumably advanced state of divine knowledge writing to Timothy wants to awake in him seeds of this knowledge: "Bring before my eyes that more perfect and more evident enlightenment which will be yours as you learn of a beauty more lovely and closer to the One. For I feel sure that my words will rekindle the sparks of God's fire which sleep in you."[24] By doing so it makes quite an explicit impression that Dionysius is certainly one who is in higher spiritual authority, even though Timothy already was a disciple of Paul before Paul traveled to

Athens, where he converted Dionysius to Christianity. It would seem that it was he, not Paul, was Timothy's divine teacher, where Paul was, perhaps, only the initiator of Timothy in Christian teaching. An additional minimization of the role of Paul can be seen not in what the corpus states, but rather in what it leaves in silence.

Even though the general outline of Pseudo-Dionysian ideas sufficiently correlates with the main propositions of Paul's sermon at the Areopagus, the author of the *CD* never explicitly refers to this sermon. Paul is not even portrayed as a member of Dionysian society. The authority of Paul and his writings are affirmed and supported,[25] while there are no references to Paul as a person with whom his supposed convert would have spent some time. The actual author of the corpus does not mention another commonly accepted fact about his historical prototype, needless to say elaborates on it: Dionysius being ordained by Paul—a fact that is commonly accepted in Christian tradition.[26]

With the exception of simply acknowledging Paul as his divine teacher and master, the author of the *CD* does not make any other references to Paul that might have made the attribution of this corpus to Dionysius the Areopagite more plausible. Pseudo-Dionysius does not mention any well-known facts about Paul from the Scriptures that might be helpful for his discourse and projection of the first-century identity—for example, Paul's encounter with Christ on the road to Damascus (Acts 9:1–19) or his ascent to the third heaven (2 Cor. 12:1–4).[27] What also is interesting is that this inclination to downplay the role of Paul is not only typical for the *CD*. There are some traces of this leaning even among the first supporters of the authenticity of the corpus. For example, Rorem and Lamoreaux observe a similar low reliance on Paul in the first commentary on the *Areopagitica*—the *Scholia* of John of Scythopolis.[28]

All of these omissions are difficult to explain if the author of the corpus intended to portray a first-century environment. However, in view of the attribution of the corpus to Dionysius the Areopagite as a literary design, historicity itself would not be the major concern. In the context of the literary design the elevated positioning of Dionysius as one among the apostles not only helps to convey an impression of apostolicity, but by purposefully shadowing the authority of Paul it also helps to elevate Dionysius to a more equal and a more independent status from Paul than the account in the Book of Acts would suggest.[29] The ministries of Paul and Dionysius present intriguing paralleled juxtapositions.

By attributing the corpus to the Areopagite as a literary device and inconspicuously promoting Dionysius to the apostolic status, our author importantly elevates the stature of the entire corpus. It helps to accentuate the content of the corpus on its own grounds independently from, or at least on equal authority with, Paul.

Paul makes references to the unknown God. Paul shows some familiarity with Greek learning, but neither in Acts nor in other books of the New Testament or Patristic tradition is Paul viewed as a philosopher himself. Dionysius the Areopagite fits better the position of the philosopher. Paul was a Jew, before his conversion a Pharisee, with profound knowledge and dedication to Judaism as his only expression of true religion. He was even one who actively persecuted Christians, which manifests the intensity of his dedication to what he considered to be the truth. Paul was also a man who was searching for verity, and when he found it in Christ he became the herald to the world about this truth.

Dionysius was an educated Greek and an Athenian judge, which also implies his profound dedication to Hellenistic philosophic and cultural values, as well as his commitment to searching for the truth both as a judge[30] and as an intellectual. He also was an "anonymous Christian," perhaps the first gentile mystically converted to Christianity, and his initial, even though not fully realized, acceptance of Christianity coincides with the climax of Christ's earthly ministry. Paul became the Jewish apostle to gentiles who helped to transmit the divine truth initially revealed in the Old Testament and later manifested in Christ to the gentile world. The Areopagite, as he is literarily depicted in the corpus, can be understood as the gentile apostle to gentiles who communicated what was true in Greek philosophy and exposed by Christ. In this role, Dionysius is conveyed as representing the apostolic witness to the divine truth of Christ (this is why his association with Peter, Bartholomew, James, the Mother of God, and especially John are important), and its essential agreement with the best of Greek philosophy. As the Old Testament, to the mind of Late Antiquity Christian, does not contradict the New Testament but proclaims the coming of Christ, the noblest of Greek wisdom testifies to the same truth affirmed by Christ. The presence of the Apostolic Fathers, and, perhaps, later Patristic authors (Clement the Philosopher as Clement of Alexandria)[31] in Dionysian society continues to serve the same line of literary reasoning. Dionysius as a fictitiously appointed author of these works, in the metaphorical significance of this application, testifies to the essential compatibility of the Christian message with the best of Greek philosophy. Therefore, it is not surprising that the most important member of the society where the divine truth of the Christian revelation and of Greek philosophy come together is the figure of Hierotheus.

Hierotheus, a name that does not have associations in the biblical and Patristic tradition,[32] is presented as the Dionysian "famous teacher" of almost, if not, greater, authority than the apostle Paul.[33] The author of the *CD* in strong terms acknowledges the divine wisdom and authority of Hierotheus and mentions sending Timothy one of Hierotheus's books, *Elements of Theology* (a work otherwise unheard of as belonging to any Patristic

58 *The Dionysian society*

author), to read.[34] The book is held in especially great esteem. The title of the book instantly brings to mind Proclus. Another work of Hierotheus mentioned and cited in the *DN* 4.14–17 is *Hymns of Love*, which also is suggestive of the Proclian *Hymns*. Of course, identification of Hierotheus with Proclus does not exhaust other possibilities. It just seems to be the most obvious one. Ilaria Ramelli, for example, believes that under the name of Hierotheus Pseudo-Dionysius disguises Origen.[35] István Perczel also extensively argues for association of the *CD* with Origenism of the fifth century.[36] Rosemary Arthur thinks that Hierotheus can be identified as a member of Jewish Hekhaloth mysticism, a Neoplatonist practitioner of theurgy, and a Christian alchemist.[37] To finish this implausible picture, one could add a Gnostic and a Manichean. In any case, the general impression about Hierotheus is that our mysterious author seems to present himself more as a disciple of Hierotheus than of Paul: Hierotheus, "who, next to the divine Paul, has been my elementary instructor."[38] Hierotheus could be next to Paul in the sense of authority, but also in the sense of temporal sequence. If the latter is true, his authority might be seen as equal to Paul, and there is evidence in the text that might support this interpretation.

Hierotheus is the most frequently named authority in the *CD*. He is to Dionysius, as Balthasar remarks, "As Socrates to Plato."[39] The influential presence of Hierotheus, or at least depicted as such, is accentuated in three main Dionysian tractates. In the *DN* our mysterious author presents a sort of commentary on Hierotheus's *Elements of Theology*,[40] he attributes to Hierotheus the idea of triadic ranking among angels in the *CH*,[41] and the Hierothean understanding of the Eucharist as the "sacrament of sacraments" is praised in the *EH*.[42] Hierotheus is the only author, apart from Scriptures, who is openly cited.[43]

Considering the level of the authority and respect that is granted to Hierotheus, it might be seen as an imprudent decision to so explicitly assign titles of the works to Hierotheus that immediately create their association with Proclus if the author of the *Areopagitica* wanted to recreate a historical environment of the apostolic period. Moreover, it is not Paul, who might be considered as the most acceptable (at least, not controversial) candidate, but Hierotheus, who is said to be with Dionysius, along with many others, including the apostle Peter and Jesus's brother James, at the Dormition of Mary.

The presence of Dionysius in the company of known New Testament figures, as has been already pointed out, has significance for promoting the elevated status of the alleged author. However, the addition of Hierotheus, a very obscure figure outside of the *CD*, to this assembly seems to be rather strange, as far as projection of the first-century contextualization might be concerned. There are, at least, two interesting details in the reference

The Dionysian society 59

to this gathering of Dionysius, Hierotheus, and other noted figures of the New Testament period for the viewing of the "life-giving and god-receiving body [τοῦ ζωαρχικοῦ καὶ θεοδόχου σώματος]"[44] of the Mother of God in the *DN* 3, as well as the general literary arrangement of this event, that might actually jeopardize the presumed recreation of the first-century environment even further. All of them have peculiar parallels in Proclus. First, Proclus's *Commentary on the Parmenides* begins with prayer, as does *DN* 3. Of course in his case Proclus invokes all gods and goddesses, including angelic choruses, benevolent daemons, and heroes to open his mind and enlighten him in comprehension of the divinely inspired mystical teaching of Plato.[45] Second, in the context of this supplication, as Stephen Gersh pointed out, Proclus "enters into contemplation with his teacher Syrianus and Plato himself . . . around 'the body' of Plato's dialogue *Parmenides*."[46] This is precisely the case with the event in the *DN* 3.

While the *DN* 3 is often viewed as a prayer that sets a proper spiritual initiation to the further detailed treatment of divine names,[47] it is actually a chapter of praise of Hierotheus as the teacher, friend, and guide of our author and second only to the authority of "the sacred writers," that is set in the context of the viewing of the "body" of the Mother of God. The emphasis of the event is not on Mary, but on Hierotheus. Being second to the authority of the authors of New Testament books, Hierotheus here also is presented as surpassing "all the divinely rapt hierarchs, all the other sacred initiators."[48] In other words, being next and second to "the sacred writers" Hierotheus actually exceeds and outshines them. The author of the *CD* clearly sets himself in a subordinate level of knowledge to Hierotheus, while more or less on an equal footing with Paul. He only wants "to analyze and with some orderly detail to expand upon the truths so briefly set down by Hierotheus" in *Elements of Theology*.[49]

This extensive reliance on Hierotheus in the corpus, however, cannot be accidental. It is more likely a part of the general literary approach where the author wants to integrate the idea of the essential congeniality between the truths of Neoplatonism and Christianity. This is why Hierotheus (Ἱερόθεος)—the name means "sanctified by God"—who more likely represents Proclus (and in him the entire Neoplatonic tradition), is included in the apostolic club, with authority that parallels the authority of Paul and in a way supersedes the authority of other sacred writers. Otherwise, the overall impression about Dionysian society is that it purposefully seems to downplay—even ignore—what is known, as little as it is, about the historical Dionysius the Areopagite, rather than to convey the first-century environment.

There is at least one more important issue related to the portrayal of apostolic and sub-apostolic environments in the *CD* that seriously undermines the credibility of the corpus to such claims or testifies to the lack of imagination or general awareness of commonly accessible historical information by the author of the *CD*. It is what Rorem calls "a shaky chronology."[50] In the early interest in the *Areopagitica*, chronological problems within the corpus were noted, but often they were simply ignored. John of Scythopolis commenting on the corpus accepts references to apostolic and sub-apostolic figures mentioned in the corpus as the proof of authenticity of the writings belonging to Dionysius of the Areopagite, but usually does not get involved with chronological issues connected with these individuals.[51]

What is known about some of the previously mentioned notable New Testament characters, and it had been known well back to Patristic times, would imply that Dionysius the Areopagite lived a quite long life—one might say, an unbelievably long life. For one thing, he outlived Timothy,[52] companion of Paul depicted in the corpus as Dionysus's own apprentice, who likely was younger than Dionysius. The chronology of his life, from his addressing a letter to the apostle John to his friendship with Polycarp and familiarity with the writings of Ignatius of Antioch, presents a really remarkable story.

In *Ep.* 7.2 he portrays himself as a contemporary of Christ and a witness to the solar eclipse at the time of Christ's crucifixion, which means he had to be at least a young adult. He ought to be in his thirties, at least, when Paul converted him to Christianity, but he lived long enough to write a letter to the apostle John (*Ep.* 10), who was exiled to Patmos. John was reportedly exiled during the persecution of Christians under the Roman emperor Domitian. Domitian became the emperor in 81 CE and reigned until his assassination in 96 CE. John of Scythopolis, with references to Irenaeus and Clement of Alexandria, places the apostle John's exile toward the last year of Domitian's reign. John of Scythopolis himself suggested that Dionysius was perhaps 25 at the time of the eclipse and around 90 when he sent his letter to apostle John.[53]

Regardless of how well aware the actual author of the *CD* was of the exact years of Domitian's reign, the number of early Patristic sources, and the well-established tradition based on these sources, presents John returning from his exile and dying a natural death in Ephesus. Our mysterious author is not unaware of this tradition, as he implies the return of John from the exile as a Dionysian personal prophetic insight: "I am completely worthy of being believed when I teach and speak the things made known about you by God, namely, that you will be released from your prison on Patmos, that you will return to the land of Asia where you will continue to act in imitation of God and will hand on your legacy to those who come after you."[54] This is not all. Dionysius the Areopagite, according to the chronology in his

The Dionysian society 61

corpus, not only prophesied the safe return of the apostle John from exile, he had to witness this return.

The recipient of the previously mentioned *Ep.* 7 was Bishop Polycarp. Polycarp of Smyrna is a likely addressee[55] and his active years as a bishop were *ca.* 96—*ca.* 156. Even if *Ep.* 7 is written around 96 CE[56] and Dionysius the Areopagite is already pushing 90, the reference in the corpus to Ignatius's *Letter to Romans*,[57] written around 107 or as late as 117, would suggest that he passed over the centennial mark and would outlive not only apostles but even most of the Apostolic Fathers. It is not surprising that John of Scythopolis was in pain to find justification for this chronological anomaly that was already pointed out in Late Antiquity. This is why John of Scythopolis places the death of Ignatius before the reign of Domitian in order to resolve the difficulty.[58]

It is hard to believe that the actual author of the *CD* was entirely unaware of these chronological discrepancies. It is equally not surprising that the authenticity of some letters (*Ep.* 6–8 and 10) and other references (*DN* 3.2–3) to Dionysian society was questioned either as to whether they were by the same author but from a different work, or were editorial insertions to prove an apostolic setting.[59] Whether it was a testimony to negligence on the part of the actual author or to later editorial interpolations of his enthusiastic readers wanting to create the impression of these works coming from the first century is hard to say. Clearly, if the actual author or his early supporters wanted to project the Areopagite's historical identity they did not do a good job.

Perczel in the context of *DN* 3.2 suggests that "'Dionysius' is not inventing a fictitious story but is encoding a real one; the gathering was that of bishops contemporary to 'Dionysius' [i.e., actual author], who are mentioned under pseudonyms."[60] The reason for such a conspiracy was to hide the real identities from unwanted censorship. Perczel's personal view of this gathering is that it might describe a council, perhaps, even the Council of Chalcedon, that the actual author of the *CD* attended. It is possible that the *CD* has some codification that is interwoven into the work. What was codified remains a mystery, however, the codification itself is not the same as intentional projection of a first-century environment. If this is the case, it is one more argument that our mysterious author did not want to produce a deliberate forgery. In at least one place, Pseudo-Dionysius even openly refers to what seems to be his own historical time when he states, "I have fallen [in description of divine names] wretchedly short not only of the theologians [authors of biblical books, including New Testament writers and apostles], their hearers and their followers but even of my own peers."[61] Here the actual author of the *CD* not only does not include himself in the

62 *The Dionysian society*

company of the apostles and New Testament authors, but excludes himself from the company of their followers, the Apostolic Fathers.

On a closer look, most of the *biographical* and *historical* remarks in the corpus appear more to jeopardize its affiliation with historical Dionysius than to support it. It is also important to point out that none of them makes any substantial contribution to the main flow of the argument. The *CD* in its content presents a more abstract and timelessly oriented perspective that does not seem to be in need of any particular historical contextualization, as such. The content of the corpus neither benefits nor suffers from the presence or absence of any biographical or personal remarks. Besides, the entire outlook of Dionysian society resonates more with contemplative semi-monastic or ascetically inclined academic settings, or even with literary style similar to the dialogues of Plato, than with anything associated with first-century Christianity. Overall, the presence of Dionysian society in the corpus, with few exceptions, leaves a sense of some artificiality rather than historicity. It is like super-structured interpolations added sporadically in the main flow of the discourse. And as we do not read Plato's *Symposium* to learn how one can stop hiccups, even though it is remarkable information and it works (most of the time),[62] the *Areopagitica* would not lose any of its significance in the absence of this imaginative society.

As far as the identity of the actual author is concerned, it is more proper to speak about intentional anonymity than pseudonymity. The author wants to stay incognito and does not leave any substantial hints in the text that might identify him. Yet he does not hide behind a historical Dionysian identity but, while remaining invisible, he uses this first-century figure as a literary device where historicity succumbs to literary significance. It is not an attempt at forgery but is rather a literary gesture. This literary gesture accentuates the symbolic nature of his writings as responding to the actual historical context in which they were written. The content of his mature reflection on many post-Nicene theological themes and advanced philosophical reflections, unthinkable in any author of the first century, is the best demonstration of actual author's intentions.

The author's appeal to the apostolic Christianity is portrayed in the *CD* from the perspective of later generations looking back on them as on founders of Christian tradition and sources of the authority, rather than intending to recreate the historical atmosphere of first-generation Christians. It is more like a literary appeal for antiquity to demonstrate the truthfulness of his statements than the attempt to associate himself as directly belonging to this antiquity. If this assumption is accurate, and attribution to the Areopagite was symbolic, then it is the irony of history that later this unintended pseudonymity, taken literally, helped first to secure the subsequent survival of the corpus and later helped to brand it as a most successful and vicious forgery. In the case of the *Areopagitica* we are dealing with a clever literary stratagem that did not intent to be a forgery.

The *CD* purposefully sets itself in the time it was composed, only appealing to the image of Dionysius the Areopagite to magnify the impact of the message it wants to portray. Otherwise, as has already been pointed out, neither the attribution to the Areopagite itself nor the presence of Dionysian society adds any significance to the main flow of its argument. The actual content of the corpus neither benefits nor suffers from the presence or absence of any biographical or personal remarks, like some parts of Plato's dialogues from various trivial chats. As the effect of metaphorical attribution to Dionysius the Areopagite increases the appreciation of the corpus's contents, the insinuation of any evidence of historical association with the first century is not only of the secondary importance, it is of no importance at all. This is the reason why the *Areopagitica* sometimes was perceived as being equipped with such a poorly managed *forgery apparatus*. The actual author did not bother with a convincing effort to present his works as coming from the first century in a historical sense. Only later, with the appearance of the *CD* on the public scene, especially, being cited in the context of ongoing Christological debates, the Areopagite attribution received an interpretation other than simply literary. The literary intention of the actual author was lost in the editorial/interpretive process to win acceptance of the corpus for a Christian audience at large, and identification of the corpus with Dionysius of the first century became accepted as historical fact. The whole idea of a literary ploy to employ the Areopagite identity as a metaphorical application succumbed to the need to secure the place of this corpus in Christian tradition.

Intensification of pseudonymity did not stop here. In the Latin transmission of the corpus Dionysius the Areopagate also happened to be confused with Dionysius of Paris (for the most part, thanks to Hilduin's *History of Saint Dionysius*),[63] and in this double identity he became the patron saint of France. John Scottus Eriugena, writing shortly after Hilduin, in the introduction to his Latin translation of the corpus, summarily reiterates the story. Eriugena narrates that Athenian Dionysius, who converted to Christianity by Paul, became his disciple and assistant. Paul consecrated him bishop of Athens. Later, at the time of Pope Clement, Dionysius visited Rome and Clement delegated him to Christianize Gaul, where Dionysius suffered martyrdom with a short miraculous afterlife interlude of cephalophory. As legend has it: "Decapitated for his faith, he nonetheless picked up his head and walked a staggering distance to his chosen site of burial, where the faithful gradually built a tomb, a church, and then an abbey."[64]

This multilayered pseudonymous heritage associated with the *Areopagitica*, even though unmasked, is still a haunting reality that distracts and clouds a more encompassing engagement with this body of works. The attribution of this corpus to Dionysius the Areopagite, literally and metaphorically understood, could better demonstrate the main intention that corresponds with focal themes of the corpus. It represents emerging Christian imperial identity in the context of inherently Hellenistic culture, where the truths of Christianity and of Greek philosophy, especially in the form of late Neoplatonism, are rather in essential agreement than in opposition. The attribution of the *CD* to this first-century Athenian convert to Christianity might express, in words of Louth, "the author's belief that the truths of Plato grasped belong to Christ, and are not abandoned by embracing faith in Christ."[65]

Notes

1 *DN* 1.1 (585B), 1.8 (597C), 3.2 (681B), 11.6, (953B); *EH* 3.3.1 (428A); *MT* 1.1 (997B); and the addressee of *DN*, *MT*; *CH*; and *EH*. In *CH* 2.5 (145C) the author of the *CD* addresses Timothy as his child, obviously implying his older age and authority.
2 Addressee of *Ep.* 9.
3 Addressee of *Ep.* 10.
4 *DN* 3.2 (681D).
5 *DN* 3.2 (681D).
6 *DN* 11.1 (949A).
7 Addressee of *Ep.* 6.
8 Addressee of *Ep.* 1–4.
9 *MT* 1.3 (1000BC). In the context of Bartholomew there is also a possible reference to his apocryphal gospel. Cf. André Wilmart and Eugène Tisserant, "Fragments grecs et latins de l'Évangile de Barthélemy," *Revue biblique* 10 (1913): 161.
10 *DN* 2.9–10 (648A-649A); 2.11 (649D); 3.2 (681AB); *CH* 6.2 (200D-201A); *EH* 2.1 (392B), etc. In *DN* 4.15–17 (713AD) Hierotheus is quoted.
11 Addressee of *Ep.* 7.
12 *DN* 5.9 (824D).
13 *DN* 4.12 (709B).
14 *Ep.* 8.6 (1097B-1100D).
15 Addressee of *Ep.* 5.
16 *DN* 8.6 (893B).
17 Addressee of *Ep.* 8.
18 *Ep.* 7.2–3 (1080A-1081C).
19 *DN* 6.2 (857A).
20 See ch. 2, I. "Dionysius the Areopagite Mentioned in the Book of Acts Is Not the Author," p. 21.
21 *DN* 3.2 (681C-684A). The text does not explicitly identify this gathering of New Testament notables as taking place around the deathbed of Mary. It has the distinct connotation of some discussion regarding the Incarnation where Hierotheus particularly distinguished himself. However, this passage explicitly indicates the presence of Mary's "life-giving and god-receiving body" that all

The Dionysian society 65

these notable figures viewed, which can imply her dormition. That this meeting took place at the time Mary "fell asleep" was already suggested by John of Scythopolis (John of Scythopolis is the earliest commentator on Pseudo-Dionysius; he lived in the sixth century, practically the contemporary of the author of the corpus; *SchDN*, PG 4:236C; PTS 62, 202–3). John of Scythopolis firmly established the tradition that both Hierotheus and Dionysius were present at the Dormition of the Mother of God. See also John Philoponus, *Prol*. PG 4:21B.

22 *Ep*. 7.2 (1081AB).
23 See, for example, *CH* 2.5 (145C), *EH* 3.3.1 (428A).
24 *EH* 7.3.11 (569A); PTS 36:132; Pseudo-Dionysius, *The Complete Works*, 259.
25 See, for example, *Ep*. 5 (1073A-1076A); and *Ep*. 7.2 (1080B).
26 Eusebius of Caesarea, *EH* 3.4.10 and 4.23.3.
27 Some possible exception can be seen in *Ep*. 5 where Pseudo-Dionysius acknowledges Paul's personal and intimate knowledge of God that might imply personal mystical experience; however, it is not explicitly said or linked to 2 Cor. 12:1–4.
28 Paul Rorem and John C. Lamoreaux, "John of Scythopolis on Apollinarian Christology and the Pseudo-Areopagite's True Identity," *Church History* 62 (1993): 480. Cf. Arthur, *Pseudo-Dionysius as Polemicist*, 3–5; Schäfer, *Philosophy of Dionysius the Areopagite*, 128.
29 This by no means diminishes the role of Pauline literature, nor discards the authority of Paul in the corpus.
30 One of the roles of the judge is to establish the truth and act justly.
31 Cf. *DN* 5.9 (824D—825A) and Clement of Alexandria, *Strom*. 8.29.1–2.
32 There are two objections to this proposition. The first objection suggested by Sheldon-Williams, who argued that Hierotheus was not a fictitious figure and pointed out one Christian bishop named Hierotheus who expressed Neoplatonic, post-Plotinian but pre-Proclian, views (I. P. Sheldon-Williams, "The ps. Dionysius and the Holy Hierotheus," *Studia Patristica* 8, part 2 (1966): 108–17). If this is the case, and Pseudo-Dionysius refers to this bishop, then his choice, first, does not help to re-create the first century apostolic milieu, it rather betrays it; second, it only supports my proposed hypothesis that the mysterious author of the *CD* did not want to present his works as belonging to historical Dionysius of the first century, but used this attribution in a literary sense. The reference to a Christian bishop who supported Neoplatonic views would additionally confirm the idea of the compatibility of what is divine in Greek philosophy with the expression of Christian revelation, which is also expressed in the corpus under literary attribution to the Areopagite. The second objection to viewing Hierotheus as a fictitious figure is the result of Dionysian influence itself. According to Eastern Orthodox tradition, Paul converted Hierotheus of Athens to Christianity along with Dionysius the Areopagite. He, like Dionysius, was a member of the Areopagus, and Paul ordained him as the first bishop of Athens. However, tradition is not clear on this point. There is a widely accepted claim that Dionysius was the first bishop of Athens, which means that Hierotheus was just a priest. Eusebius of Caesarea with reference to Dionysius of Corinth mentions Dionysius the Areopagite as the first bishop of Athens, see *EH* 3.4.10 and 4.23.3. In any case, Hierotheus died in the first century as a martyr, his feast day is October 17 (October 4, old style).
33 *DN* 2.9–10 (648AC); 3.2 (681A).
34 *DN* 3.2 (681B).

66 *The Dionysian society*

35 Ramelli, *The Christian Doctrine of Apokatastasis*, 694–96; for the entire discussion of the mystery of Pseudo-Dionysius, his lost writings and Hierotheus see, 694–721.
36 See, for example, Perczel, "Ps. Dionysius and Palestinian Origenism," in *The Sabaite Heritage in the Orthodox Church*, ed. Joseph Patrich (Louvain: Peeters Publishers, 2001), 261–82.
37 Arthur, *Pseudo-Dionysius as Polemicist*, 28, 34, and 37.
38 *DN* 3.2 (681A).
39 Balthasar, "Denys," 2:150n17.
40 *DN* 3.2–3.
41 *CH* 6.2 (200D), and as Louth observes, "No Christian writer before Denys produces this doubly threefold pattern," (Louth, *Denys the Areopagite*, 37).
42 *EH* 3.1 (424C).
43 *DN* 4.15–17.
44 *DN* 3.2 (681CD); PTS 33:141.
45 *In Parm.* 1 (617.1–618.20).
46 Gersh, "The Pseudonymity of Dionysius the Areopagite and the Platonic Tradition," 106.
47 Schäfer, *Philosophy of Dionysius the Areopagite*, 76.
48 *DN* 3.2 (681D); PTS 33:141; Pseudo-Dionysius, *The Complete Works*, 70.
49 *DN* 3.3 (684D); PTS 33:143; Pseudo-Dionysius, *The Complete Works*, 71. See also, *DN* 2.9–10. Cf. Rorem, *Pseudo-Dionysius: A Commentary*, 146–47.
50 Rorem, *Pseudo-Dionysius: A Commentary*, 13.
51 See, Rorem and Lamoreaux, *John of Scythopolis and the Dionysian Corpus*, 100–2; cf. Stang, *Apophasis and Pseudonymity in Dionysius the Areopagite*, 20.
52 *Ep.* 9.1 (1104B). Timothy as the first bishop of Ephesus (Eusebius of Caesarea, *HE* 3.4.5), according to the fourth century *Acta S. Timothei*, was martyred by pagans in 97 CE. Intriguingly enough, as Campbell notes, "Both of the *Hierarchies* [addressed to Timothy as the recipient] have references to the writings of St. John. His Gospel was not written till after the death of Timothy" (Campbell, "Introduction," in Dionysius the Pseudo-Areopagite, *The Ecclesiastical Hierarchy*, 7).
53 John of Scythopolis, *SchEp*, PG 4:573BD, see, Rorem and Lamoreaux, *John of Scythopolis and the Dionysian Corpus*, 101–2.
54 *Ep.* 10 (1120A); PTS 36:209–10; Pseudo-Dionysius, *The Complete Works*, 289. Of course, there is an alternative possibility in addressing this letter to the apostle John, proposed by John Copp. According to Copp, the actual author of the corpus wanted some Hellenistically inclined Christians to keep hope that in the state's confrontational position toward pagan learning institutions, these institutions would survive. "In this letter, Dionysius may have been trying to negotiate between sensitive Christians and speculative Neo-Platonists. The letter prophesies recovery. As John would return to Asia with his deep understanding of Christ, strong, steady minds would return to the schools with valuable insights" (Copp, *Dionysius the Pseudo-Areopagite*, 145).
55 However, the content of the letter is very distant from the milieu of Polycarp of Smyrna.
56 The earliest approximate year of Polycarp's activity and the year of Domitian's death, a possible year when the apostle John was exiled on Patmos and as such the most appropriate year for the Dionysian *Ep.* 10.
57 *DN* 4.12 (709B).

The Dionysian society 67

58 John of Scythopolis, *SchDN*, PG 4:264BC. Cf. Saffrey, "New Objective Links Between the Pseudo-Dionysius and Proclus," 66–67.
59 See Brons, "Sekundäre Textparteien im Corpus Pseudo-Dionysiacum?" 5:99–140; Nasta, "Quatre Etats de la Textualité dans l'Histoire du Corpus Dionyseinne," 31–65. Cf. Pseudo-Dionysius, *The Complete Works*, 69n127, 266n14 and 288n152; Arthur, *Pseudo-Dionysius as Polemicist*, 128.
60 Perczel, "The Earliest Syriac Reception of Dionysius," 29; and endnote 11 on page 37. Cf. Arthur, *Pseudo-Dionysius as Polemicist*, 190–91.
61 *DN* 13.4 (981C); PTS 33:230; Pseudo-Dionysius, *The Complete Works*, 130.
62 See Plato, *Symp.* 185ce.
63 Hilduin, however, contrary to what was long believed, did not invent many hagiographical stories that became "classical" elements of Dionysian "biography" (including the conflation of Dionysius the Areopagite with Dionysius of Paris). There are traces of them in previous *vitae*. Hilduin, though, effectively elaborated on them to give them form, both in prose and in poetry, which captivated the popular imagination for centuries. See Marianne M. Delaporte, "He Darkens Me with Brightness: The Theology of Pseudo-Dionysius in Hilduin's Vita of Saint Denis," *Religion & Theology* 13 (2006): 220–21.
64 Rorem, *Pseudo-Dionysius: A Commentary*, 15.
65 Louth, *Denys the Areopagite*, 11.

5 The metaphorical symbolism of the attribution

The notion that Pseudo-Dionysius was a Neoplatonic Christian, the most obvious impression that comes from an unbiased reading of the corpus, usually downplayed for various ideological reasons by Dionysian scholars, actually might help toward appreciation of the content of the corpus. Platonic and Neoplatonic influence and language had already become a part of Christian discourse long before Pseudo-Dionysius. However, the influence of Greek philosophy on Patristic writers, including our mysterious author, first of all was far more complex than simply Christian theology borrowing from and depending on Greek philosophy. Second, this influence by no means diminishes the originality and distinctiveness of Christian writers. Third, it is inaccurate to speak about the Hellenization of Christianity as though this operated in only one direction. It is also legitimate to speak about the Christianization of Hellenism. It was not merely Christian fathers who were directly or indirectly influenced by Hellenistic philosophy. Some pagan philosophers demonstrated comprehensive familiarity with Christianity already in the ante-Nicene period. All pagan philosophers in one or another form were affected by Christianity after it acquired, first, legalized status under Constantine, then in a higher degree when it became the state religion of the Roman Empire under Theodosius I. In other words, the influence was interactively mutual, which cannot be otherwise with two ideological systems coexisting in the same cultural and social environment for several centuries. Here we are not only speaking about simple familiarity of Christian thinkers with Greek philosophy and pagan intellectuals with Christianity. It also was a dialogue of ideas. For example, in Alexandria, the Neoplatonically inclined female philosopher Hypatia (d. 415), who suffered a brutal death by the hands of a Christian mob in one of Alexandrian riots, had among her disciples the Christian Synesius of Cyrene (ca. 370—ca. 413), who later became a married bishop of Ptolemais. Another Alexandrian non-Christian Neoplatonic teacher, Hierocles (active in the first half of the fifth century), had a Christian student Aeneas (d. ca. 518) who became the founder of the Christian philosophical school in Gaza. Hierocles's own philosophy was more pronouncedly "monotheistic" than that of his pagan colleagues.[1] The non-Christian philosopher Ammonius (ca. 435/445–517/526), also teaching in Alexandria, had among his students John Philoponus, one of early supporters of the authenticity of the *Areopagitica*, and Zacharias Scholasticus (d. after 536), who became a bishop of Mytilene and authored the *Life of Severus*.[2] Even in the period of quite intense crackdowns by ecclesiastical and imperial powers on paganism, philosophical and Neoplatonical exchange between pagan and Christian intellectuals persisted.

What is most important is that, as the consequence of this interaction, already before the sixth century, being Hellenized did not necessarily mean being anti-Christian—it meant to be civilized.[3] Both Christian and non-Christian inhabitants of the Byzantine Empire are essentially the product of a single overarching culture. The role of Neoplatonism in this context is remarkable. Neoplatonism was not a *secularized* discipline of philosophy in our modern sense. In Plotinus, philosophy reached a state in which it had become a religion, and religion had become a contemplative philosophy. If for Plotinus it still remained a religion of philosophers, Iamblichus introduced a significant shift toward synthesis of philosophical, cultic, and popular religious elements, under the unifying umbrella of Neoplatonism. Access to the ultimate invisible reality, or participation in the Divine, was realized not only in ascetically oriented contemplation but also through ritualistic, theurgically interpreted sacramentality. In this instance, Neoplatonism was not a religion only for the Hellenistic intellectual elite. It became a rather complex cultural phenomenon of a religiously formed system of metaphysics with significant soteriological implications that combined popular ritualistic and mythic elements. As such, late Neoplatonism was not simply a school of thought that existed alongside or in opposition to Christianity. It was rather a characteristic of Hellenistic cultural expression that in the late Roman Empire was penetrating all layers of social life and, in one or another form, influencing all religious groups. Furthermore, if, for Plotinus and Iamblichus, asceticism was set predominantly by their personal example and was not necessarily required of their pupils, in Proclus asceticism emerges in its institutionalized semi-monastic form.[4]

For Late Antiquity Christians, who, along with their non-Christian contemporaries, would understand philosophy as a search for the true knowledge of things eternal and divine, philosophy would represent a way of life and the content of basic human, divinely oriented, knowledge. From both Christian and non-Christian perspectives, "philosophy" would not differ from what could be understood as the quest for perfection, virtue, self-control, happiness, and knowledge of God. The name "philosophy" becomes applicable to the Christian religion itself. Thus, philosophy as a search for the Divine for many Christians, including Pseudo-Dionysius, is the ideal of ascetic life that combines aspects of contemplation and virtue or *theoria* and *praxis*. In this regard, again, it is not significantly different in its main methodological and teleological aspects from non-Christian asceticism. Nevertheless, the philosophical and ascetic orientation in Christian writings indicates not so much a wide-open reception of unfiltered pagan philosophy into Christian discourse, but broadly used literary, conceptual, and thematic elements of philosophy for their own purposes. Operating with similar concepts, pagans and Christians frequently expressed fundamental differences. Their agendas and starting premises are also often different.

It is likewise misleading to view Christian and pagan asceticism as homogeneous trends in themselves or in their relationship to each other. Having its source in popular morality and philosophical language makes any form of asceticism a complex phenomenon.[5] At the same time, the presence of similar literary genres, shared methodological principles, similarities in ontological, metaphysical, and epistemological perspectives in Christian and pagan literature is an intricate feature encompassing cultural development that characterizes Late Antiquity where it is impossible to draw a precise line between explicitly pagan and Christian components.

An additional important factor is that Christianity and Neoplatonism are both essentially monotheistic, *if*, of course, as Armstrong remarks, "One is prepared to admit that there can be more than one kind of monotheism."[6] The influence of Platonic metaphysics on Christian theology could be seen in the Christian understanding of the unchangeability and transcendence of God. Similarly with Platonism, Patristic theology viewed visible things only as distant and imperfect representations of the ultimately invisible reality of the spiritual realm, which were granted a primary significance in the interpretation of ontological causality, which also had considerable influence on Christian spirituality.[7]

Pseudo-Dionysius addressed the paradoxes of his time. More than any other philosophically inclined Christian writer of Late Antiquity, the author of the *Areopagitica* attempted to reconcile intricacies between what is Hellenistic and what is Christian. His laborious and deliberate mix of scriptural, Patristic, and philosophic ideas confirms the congeniality of those materials with the ultimate source of the truth, or at least they were considered to be congenial to his mind. The *CD* significantly contributes to the lowering if not eliminating of boundaries between Hellenized and Christian cultural identities. The best of Hellenistic philosophy was utilized to express a pronouncedly Christian worldview.

For a significant number of educated aristocracy, which showed the most resistance to Christianization and on whom the Roman Empire depended for filling in administrative positions in the government, the adherence to paganism was rooted in centuries-long social convention where Hellenistic religion was not only a matter of tradition but also a manifestation of their "loyalty to the Roman State."[8] In this regard, especially in the context of the intensified anti-pagan campaign of Justinian, the *CD* can be seen as addressing issues pertaining to the aristocracy's concerns, issues that would allow preserving their traditional, elevated, richly ritualized status. Pseudo-Dionysius contributes to consolidation of a Christian idea of loyalty to the state and development of a Christian idea of monarchy that became the dominant governing principle in Eastern and Western Christendom for many centuries.

At the same time Pseudo-Dionysius might have intentions to limit the power and involvement of imperial figures in the affairs of the Church, which could apply in the cases of Zeno, Justin, and especially Justinian. The theological interests of Justinian and his imperial power made him, at least in his own mind, the final arbiter of political and religious issues. His grand-scaled reforms and his vision of Christian Roman Empire was the vision of the determined individual who would not stop or concede before he achieves what he wants. The hierarchical order of the Dionysian system established a different worldview where among all levels of the metaphysical stratification nothing is said about political power and its role in the sacred arrangement of the world. The Dionysian emphasis is not on *sacralization* of imperial power but on *ecclesiation* of social order.

It would not be entirely correct, though, to suggest that the *Areopagitica* is devoid of any important implications, albeit being often rather codified than explicitly stated, of political theory. Hathaway makes a convincing case for Pseudo-Dionysius in *Ep.* 8 to parallel Socrates's discussion on the judgment of the souls in Plato's *Gorgias*.[9] In Hathaway's opinion, our anonymous author substitutes Demophilus for Plato's Callicles and demonstrates through the Carpus's story (*Ep.* 8.6) the Platonic distinction between reason and desire. The vocabulary of the letter shows that Pseudo-Dionysius was directly familiar with dialogues of Plato and draws a significant amount of his material from Proclus's commentaries on the *First Alcibiades*, *Republic*, *Gorgias*, and *Phaedrus*, the latter two of which are now lost. This for Hathaway places the author of the *CD* among Proclus's students and makes the actual content of the letter only marginally Christian. Thus, we have another Pseudo-Dionysian trick uncovered. Unless we agree with Hathaway's suggestion that Damascius was the actual author of the *CD*, this conspiratorial Platonic encoding of *Ep.* 8 does not introduce anything of additional importance. The Neoplatonism of Pseudo-Dionysius is obvious, just as is his intimate familiarity with Christian Scriptures that is not manifested to the same degree in extant works of Damascius.

72 *The metaphorical symbolism*

It is convincing, however, to agree with Hathaway that *Ep.* 8 and to some degree *Ep.* 9 are the only ones in the entire corpus that shed light on Dionysian political theory, the problem of justice, and their relation to his hierarchic order.[10] *Ep.* 8 might also give some indications of the need and purpose of his writings: to communicate a strong sense of the organized, orderly, and sacred structure of society. However, Pseudo-Dionysius would not be alone among Christians to voice his protest against the unruly activities of some monks in those turbulent times, and his call for a more pronounced expression of Christian love and toleration, for the toleration, at least, among rival Christian groups in the course of aggressive Christianization and cultural transformation.[11]

What makes the *Areopagitica* a unique product of its own time is that it represents an explicit, deliberate, and original speculative synthesis of late Neoplatonism with Christian tradition. This innovative and synergetic synthesis in a mysteriously enigmatic form, lays the foundation, and characterizes better than anything else, the nature of Byzantine culture, social order, governance, and theology. The sophisticated incorporation of Neoplatonic elements into a Christian context would serve as an important component in securing an ultimate transition from the Old Way, with all its aspirations dear to the heart of an educated and common Hellenized person, and the customs associated with the establishment of the New Way of imperial Byzantine Christian identity. George Fedotov correctly identifies Pseudo-Dionysius as "the first word of Byzantinism."[12] As such, the *Areopagitica* is an important step in the crystallization of the idea of Christendom with the emphasis on predominantly sacramental ecclesial stratification in close conformity to the angelic orders and thus to God. It is the foundational work for finalizing the formation of the civilized Roman-Byzantine Christian identity. The identity that continued the cultural standards of Hellenistic antiquity understood itself as complying with the notion of an uninterrupted succession of Christian tradition.[13] To be a true and loyal citizen of the Roman Empire was to be culturally a Hellenistic Christian. The *Areopagitica* not only helped to make this transition, but by uniting the final expression of Neoplatonism with Christianity as a congenial whole, it contributed to probably the unprecedented historical continuation of Western civilization: its uninterrupted existence from Ancient Greece to present time.

The *CD* is a theoretical, paradigm-forming, speculatively visionary work in touch with its own time and with a focus on the future. The *Areopagitica* did not simply attempt to analyze what was going on, but predominantly intended to find an effective resolution of numerous tensions that involved issues of cultural and worldview perspectives. The effectiveness of the Dionysian vision proved to be successful. In a time of turbulence and drastic transitions and paradigm shifts, a new, assuring, instructive, summa-like didactic work was needed. More than anything else the *CD* in its content provided the ground and the justification for Christians educated in Greek *paideia* to continue their appreciation for Hellenistic learning and culture, and to preserve the general outlines of Hellenistic worldview. It is, perhaps, why some Christian intellectuals so easily ignored the suspicious origin and schematic artificiality of metaphysical constructions of explicitly Neoplatonic orientation of the corpus: it gave them a legitimate excuse to preserve the best of philosophic tradition as a reflection of their cultural mentality in Christianized form and continue pursuing their philosophic interests. In this context there is a certain logic in attributing those highly philosophical and deeply theoretical treatises to the pen of Dionysius the Areopagite, however, not as a pretentious forgery but as a literary ploy.

This attribution is an emblematic act in itself. Under the name of the Areopagite, Byzantines could perceive a symbolic reconciliation between Athens and Jerusalem in a mutually inclusive Christian Greco-Roman identity. Where Dionysian influence expresses the most significance is in reinforcement of the sense of connection and continuity with the past. The *CD* introduced and, by metaphorical attribution to the apostolic times, justified the validity of Christian faith in accord with the cultural norms that would characterize a person as civilized. The metaphysical structure in Pseudo-Dionysius is important for the distinctly Christian expression of the Hellenistic and Neoplatonic worldview.[14] It provides the background for the essential cultural stability in transition to imperial Christian identity that became the intellectual pattern that incontestably governed the worldview of Western Christianity until the Renaissance and still governs religious aspects of the Eastern Orthodox worldview. Here is one of the *Areopagitica*'s main contributions. His subsidiary contributions can be seen against excesses in the Origenism or other -isms of the time that were customarily associated with some Patristic authority such as disproportionate emphasis on the role of individual apart from hierarchical ecclesiastical (i.e., divinely guided, structured, and communal development), affirming the mystery of God (apophatic theology) against endless Christological debates of all sorts and camps, and so on.

The Dionysian corpus in Rutledge's assessment "presents what is in effect a complete synthesis of cosmology, anthropology and theology, in which the things of this world are seen in their proper proportion, and true significance."[15] Obviously while addressing and presenting his main perspective of theocentric cosmic and social reality, Pseudo-Dionysius also makes allusions to peripheral topics. About some of the topics we might only guess, some are more explicitly stated, but if they are taken out of the *Areopagitica*'s main context they do not constitute the kernel of Dionysian exposition.

Accusations proposed toward the *Areopagitica*, both coming from antiquity and modern scholarship, for example, scrutinizing this corpus as the most apparent forgery in order to secure views associated with Monophysitism, Apollinarianism, Origenism, or simply a hidden subversion of Christianity into Neoplatonism, testify not so much to a confused body of writings as to a complex one. Yes, it is true that there are number of issues where the *CD* is rather ambiguous, and the reasons for such ambiguity are not apparent. However, while concentrating on what Pseudo-Dionysius does not state with more or less clarity these endless searches for what is wrong and troubling in the *CD* seem to miss what is most obvious. What is obvious is the spiritual and philosophical content of the corpus, the topics that are discussed with detailed precision.

Some of these topics might not be comfortable for modern perceptions of what Christian tradition should be, but the main content of the corpus and its subsequently formative influence are the most important factors that secured the survival of these writings, rather than their affiliation with Dionysius the Areopagite. In this regard, it might be useful to refresh the long-ago suggested but forgotten estimations of the basic importance of the corpus. Already before Koch's and Stiglmayr's definitive discoveries, Brooke Westcott, for example, thought that the *CD* was a definitely pseudonymous work, but not necessarily a forgery. The contents of the corpus were based on Christian Scripture and tradition, but not on the authority of its attribution to Dionysius the Areopagite.[16] More recently Thomas Campbell, in the introduction to his translation of the *EH*, offers a supportive suggestion, similar in tone and with reference to Westcott:

> Nevertheless, though in all probability the writings are pseudonymous, there is no reason to consider them a forgery. The historical dress is of meager texture. The author rests his argument on Scripture and Tradition and reason, not on his own authority. Nothing was more natural than that a later writer, himself greatly influenced by Greek philosophy, should adopt the one name in the New Testament which combined Greek culture with Christian faith. The adoption of the particular title of Dionysius the Areopagite is significant. It was not opposed to the practice of the age, wherein a representative name would describe the spirit and object of the writer, and would not be in itself a sign of willful dishonesty.[17]

The pseudonymous nature of the corpus and the historically shaky association of it with Dionysius the Areopagite was suspected for a long time until it was definitely proven, but this is not the issue of the significance of the *Areopagitica* and why it expressed such tremendous influence. The acceptance of this shaky association with the Areopagite was more an excuse than the main driving force for the corpus to express its influence. As Golitzin correctly remarks, "Pseudonymity in the ancient church only worked when it expressed the common mind."[18]

Besides, what Pseudo-Dionysius attempted to do was not different from what other Christian intellectuals did throughout the Patristic and especially Medieval periods—that is, to find a common ground between Greek philosophy and Christian theology. There is, however, one important nuance. If, during the Middle Ages, Western Christian theologians articulated the doctrine of a double truth, one philosophic and another from revelation, in Pseudo-Dionysius we encounter more the agreement than the dilemma between the two. Dionysian vocabulary and his intellectual background present at times a puzzling and eclectic consortium of Neoplatonic and Patristic ideas, interwoven into creative, later proven to become very influential, discourse. The fact of the corpus's influence indicates some sort of appropriateness of such an enterprise. He genuinely and quite openly incorporated Neoplatonic and Christian elements into an enigmatic fabric of symbolic significance.

During the late Patristic period and the emergence of a distinctly Byzantine pattern on the East, and later the emergence of Scholasticism in the West, Greek philosophy remained an important, although not uncontroversial, component of Christian theological discourse. It does not matter that Plato yielded to Aristotle in the High Middle Ages,[19] Greek philosophy nevertheless was an integral part, and Neoplatonism never entirely went out of fashion. Hence, it is not surprising that the *CD* was held in high regard. It was not the name of the author that was the driving force maintaining interest in the corpus. Naturally, the apostolic association of the alleged author helped to ease some possible scruples or doubts about the origin of these works that periodically visited critical minds of leading intellectuals for centuries.[20] The presence of Christian material in its content and the overall Christian orientation of the corpus were also important factors for the acceptance of the corpus.[21]

Precisely because this corpus was not designed as an intended forgery, the name of Dionysius the Areopagite, and not any other established Patristic authority, was chosen. It is an indication of a calculated literary ploy. Dionysian attribution, especially assessed on the internal evidence from the text, first, does not really suggest depiction of the historical New Testament period; second, it successfully shields the actual author from any hints to his identity. At the same time, designation of this corpus to the Areopagite communicates the importance of this affiliation not as in a historical, but in a metaphoric sense. The author did not want simply to hide under the mask of established authority to secure the survival of his works and to increase the readership. He or she purposefully selected an obscure figure from the first century to emphasize the symbolism of this attribution and to accentuate the message that he, or she, wanted to convey. The metaphorical significance of assigning Dionysius as the author goes hand in hand with the symbolism employed within the corpus. Dionysius the Areopagite is both known and unknown. He is known as the New Testament individual converted to Christianity by Paul, and at the same time unknown apart from some sparse hagiographical references. Not in a supposed historicity of the corpus, but in what this name might *represent* is this attribution justified. One of reasons for the futility of the search for the identity of the author, in addition to meager external historical evidence, is its misplaced emphasis on the presupposed ascription of the corpus to historical Dionysius. Treating the Dionysian ascription as a literary device makes it more transparent why any searches for any historical figure that might have been behind its authorship would not lead to conclusive results.

The actual author did not want to impose these writings as if they were coming from the first century. He wanted to draw attention to his message. It was not the name of the alleged author as the content of the *CD* that was the main attraction. The influence of the *Areopagitica* is the great testimony that the corpus managed to address the most important aspects in the formation of Christian Roman-Byzantine identity. It contributed to what would become a traditional exposition of Christian metaphysics where cosmological, ecclesial, and liturgical aspects are closely connected with an epistemological and mystical perspective within the overarching theocentric explication. The *CD* adequately addressed important issues of the time by providing reflections for formation of the main pattern that was in the process of its formation. It was the right body of literature produced at the right time. Only later, when the need to establish the grounds for wider acceptance of the corpus presented itself, was that literary affiliation transformed into a historical one, thus replacing the literary attribution into pseudo-historical and creating the pretext for still-hunting pseudonymity.

Notes

1 Wallis, *Neoplatonism*, 139, 142–43.
2 Athanassiadi, "Introduction," in Damascius, *The Philosophical History*, 22.
3 In one instance Gregory of Nazianzus praises Hellenistic qualities as Christian and contrasts them to barbarism, *Ep.* 62, GCS 53:57.
4 Polymnia Athanassiadi, "Persecution and Response in Late Paganism," 10–11.
5 See Anthony Meredith, "Asceticism: Christian and Greek," *Journal of Theological Studies* 27 (1976): 313–14, 330–32.
6 A. H. Armstrong, "Plotinus and Christianity," in *Platonism in Late Antiquity*, eds. Stephen Gersh and Charles Kannengiesser (Notre Dame, IN: University of

Notre Dame Press, 1992), 124. As Proclus, for example, in one place remarks, "For every god is god by virtue of the One, though the supreme God is one purely and simply, having no multiple aspects." *In Parm.* 1.641–42, *Procli Commentarium in Platonis Parmenidem*, ed. Victor Cousin (Hildesheim, Germany: Georg Olms Verlag, 1961), 641–42; *Proclus' Commentary on Plato's Parmenides*, trans. Glenn R. Morrow and John M. Dillon (Princeton, NJ: Princeton University Press, 1987), 36. Cf. *In Tim.* 5.302E. See also, John Kenney, "Monotheism and Polytheistic Elements in Classical Mediterranean Spirituality," in *Classical Mediterranean Spirituality*, ed. A. H. Armstrong (New York, NY: Crossroad Publishing, 1986), 289; Michael Frede, "Monotheism and Pagan Philosophy in Later Antiquity," in *Pagan Monotheism in Late Antiquity*, eds. Polymnia Athanassiadi and Michael Frede (Oxford: Clarendon Press, 1999), 41–67. It should also be noted that the word "monotheistic" or "monotheism" cannot be applied to Neoplatonism in the literal sense as a belief in existence of only one god. Monotheism, in this context, rhetorically emphasizes the existence of single and unique ontological and metaphysical principle.
7 See C. J. de Vogel, "Platonism and Christianity," 27–28, 47.
8 Cyril Mango, *Byzantium: The Empire of the New Rome* (London: Phoenix, 2005), 89.
9 Hathaway, *Hierarchy and the Definition of Order*, 93–99.
10 Hathaway, *Hierarchy and the Definition of Order*, chapter 4, esp. pp. 85–93.
11 *Ep.* 8.5 (1097A).
12 George P. Fedotov, *The Russian Religious Mind: Kievan Christianity: The 10th to the 13th Centuries* (New York, NY: Harper Torchbooks, 1960), 27.
13 Even Golitzin recognizes the Dionysian contribution to the formation of Roman Christian imperial identity as "a side effect" of the *CD*'s influence, *Mystagogy*, 397–99.
14 Cf. Schäfer, *Philosophy of Dionysius the Areopagite*, 163–71.
15 Denys Rutledge, *Cosmic Theology: The Ecclesiastical Hierarchy of Pseudo-Denys: An Introduction* (London: Routledge and Kegan Paul, 1964), 4.
16 Brooke Westcott, "Dionysius the Areopagite," *Contemporary Review* 5 (1867): 7.
17 Campbell, "Introduction," in Dionysius the Pseudo-Areopagite, *The Ecclesiastical Hierarchy*, 11. Cf. Westcott, "Dionysius the Areopagite," 8.
18 Golitzin, *Et Introibo Ad Altare Dei*, 8.
19 It should be noted that the *CD* already demonstrates significant methodological reliance on Aristotle.
20 See, for example, Schäfer, *Philosophy of Dionysius the Areopagite*, 13–14; Kenneth Paul Wesche, "Christological Doctrine and Liturgical Interpretation in Pseudo-Dionysius," *St. Vladimir's Theological Quarterly* 33 (1989): 72; Hathaway, *Hierarchy and the Definition of Order in the Letters of Pseudo-Dionysius*, 21; etc.
21 Louth, "The Reception of Dionysius up to Maximus the Confessor," 51–52.

Conclusion

There are as many keys to unlock the enigma of the *CD* as key holders; however, for the most part none of them works perfectly. Apart from the openly unfriendly reception of the corpus in modern scholarship as either a wicked forgery or an unmasked non-Christian Neoplatonism devoid of any genuinely Christian content, a growing number of Dionysian students still unceasingly attempt to elucidate both its mysterious origin and no less mysterious identity of the author. At least, they try to explain why these works were attributed to Dionysius the Areopagite. Lack of any specific information that can with some certainty identify the anonymous author still makes Dionysian scholars unsettled and their results ambiguous, if not implausible.

Endre von Ivánka believes that the key for mystery of the corpus in its author's desire to fill the otherwise hollow structure of late Neoplatonism with Christian content. In such a way the corpus attains the highest quality of apologetic Christian literature and serves as an effective tool of what now might be called *evangelical outreach*.[1] Ronald Hathaway, and those who followed him, sees it the other way around. In Hathaway's view the *Areopagitica*, hastily composed by the last head of Athenian Academy, Damascius, becomes the hiding place for an otherwise persecuted pagan philosophy, helping this form of philosophy to survive (albeit be it in Christian cloth) frightening extinction.[2]

As far as the view of the *Areopagitica* as a sort of apologetic endeavor to present Christianity in an acceptable and convincing way to non-Christian intellectuals is concerned, there is no point denying the apologetic aspect of the corpus as, for example, was done by Balthasar.[3] But was late Neoplatonism really so bankrupt a system of thought as Ivánka wants to suggest, or is it presented as such in the corpus? Schäfer,[4] Perl,[5] and Wear and Dillon[6] show in their research that this was not the case. Besides, how much evidence for the success of the *CD* in the conversion of pagan intellectuals to Christianity do we have? Similarly, the argument of Hathaway, who sees the

Areopagitica as a disguised pagan Neoplatonism and proposes Damascius as the author, lacks evidence. Is the *CD* only a bare exposition of Neoplatonic philosophy under the mere facade of Christian teaching? If this is the case, it makes Damascius a great biblical and Patristic scholar, as well as an expert trinitarian theologian.

The idea that the *Areopagitica* aimed to convert pagans to Christianity by intellectual means was already suggested by John of Scythopolis in the *Prologue* to his *Scholia* on the corpus.[7] In the case of John of Scythopolis it *certainly* was an apologetic effort, not one to convert pagans to Christianity, but to secure the acceptance of the corpus in the Christian community. John of Scythopolis also minimizes the importance of Hierotheus in the *CD* in favor of Dionysius's relation to Paul and, according to Rorem and Lamoreaux, occasionally provides biblical annotations for vocabulary and concepts that might be associated with Neoplatonism.[8] The bottom line is that both the notion of Pseudo-Dionysius as a Christian apologist writing to educated Christians and the idea of Pseudo-Dionysius as Damascius hiding his Neoplatonism in a Christian box in order to preserve it are very unlikely scenarios. However, the kernel of truth behind those suggestions is that the *CD* is essentially a Neoplatonic work.

Among other allegedly miraculous keys, for Alexander Golitzin the key to the *CD* is the clever attempt to curtail the otherwise destructive tendencies of some monastic communities in the East, especially in Syria, that believed that their monastic authority derived from prophets and spiritual sages of the past and was not subordinated to ecclesiastical hierarchy. Thus, only a monastic and mystagogical reading of the *Areopagitica* unlocks its mystery. Hans Urs von Balthasar treats the author's pseudonymity as a spiritual identification with the historical Dionysius the Areopagite, hence making this pseudonymity both justifiable and legitimate. Charles Stang suggests cracking the Dionysian enigma through an exclusively Pauline reading of the corpus. These are just a few examples. Each of them expresses a different level of plausibility. All of them manifest a high degree of creativity, mixed with great scholarship and imagination. These attempts are useful and they, indeed, help us to understand the Dionysian corpus better. One of the main weaknesses of them all is that they only address one particular aspect, or one particular set of issues, of the corpus, sometime with evidence from the text, sometimes only with meager references between the lines. At the same time, they either totally ignore or drastically downplay other, no less important evidence that comes directly from the text, this in spite of the fact that the majority of modern Dionysian scholars endorse an integrative approach—they propose to treat the *CD* as one organic and internally connected body of writings.

It would be an oversimplification to view the *CD* as aimed only at promoting or arguing against one particular issue or out of one particular set of circumstances (whatever they might be, based on the specific preference of any individual scholar), laying aside everything else. The *CD* was written in a complex historical, political, and theological environment. Naturally, the complexity of this context reflected itself in the corpus. The purposively clandestine nature of the corpus makes identification of this context even more problematic; nevertheless, threads of evidence occasionally surface, mostly in contextualized form, and with the meticulous efforts of numerous scholars were, with more or less precision, identified. However, it is also an oversimplification to attempt to reconstruct or identify *one* element of Pseudo-Dionysian context, to which the corpus might bear only implicit and unclear references, to see this element as the main driving force that prompted our anonymous author to write. For example, it is possible that Pseudo-Dionysius was familiar and disagreed with Stephen Bar Sudhaili, assuming with Rosemary Arthur that Stephen Bar Sudhaili's *Book of the Holy Hierotheos* was written earlier than the *Areopagitica*, but not in response to it as was thought before.[9] It is possible that some aspects of this disagreement found their place in the *CD*. However, would those points of disagreement constitute the main force behind the content of the whole Pseudo-Dionysian corpus, as Rosemary Arthur suggests?[10] It is very unlikely. If, as Arthur notes, "There is no evidence that Bar Sudhaili knew Greek,"[11] then, why would Pseudo-Dionysius be writing against him in Greek, masterfully and purposefully hiding his, presumably, Syriac identity?

    The unsettling effect of the author's anonymity was felt no differently in Late Antiquity as it is in modern scholarship. There is a particular similarity between some modern and late antique approaches to the *Areopagitica*. Many ancient critics (or defenders) of the *CD*, like modern critics (or defenders), were looking for evidence to explain the enigmatic corpus. If in contemporary research, efforts were made to search for some hidden hints and specific colloquialisms to pinpoint either the geographical milieu or the historical background of the actual author, and from those often speculative and inconclusive findings to construct the whole edifice of a solution for the Dionysian question, ancient critics had the advantage of more immediate historical context. The *CD* was produced in closer proximity to their own historical, cultural, and intellectual circumstances. Therefore, Proclian Neoplatonism was not an unfamiliar issue in their view of the corpus, as it was for modern scholarship until the break of the twentieth century (however, it was equally controversial). Nevertheless, this historical immediacy still did not solve the enigmatic nature of the otherwise unknown works, and an effort was made to find allusions that could help to identify either the author or his theological inclinations. Hence, the actual author of the *CD* was attacked as Monophysite, Apollinarian, Origenist, or defended as Chalcedonian and orthodox. In both instances, late antique and modern, most

Conclusion 81

of the debate around the *Areopagitica* was around uncertainties and ambiguities, in an intense search for clandestine clues and in the construction of definitive hypotheses out of scant or simply guessed evidence.

As Andrew Louth observes, "Our author never steps aside from his pseudonym to give us a chance to see why he adopted it."[12] It is not even the pseudonymity as the anonymity, or what more adequately can be termed the *unsettling effect of anonymity*, that was the driving force, which was only settled in antiquity after the appeal of the main content of the *CD* prevailed and won the day. Only after the apostolicity of the *Areopagitica* was accepted, its uncontested influence flourished, as well as its important impact on Eastern Christianity and Western civilization. The futility of some modern research might be falling into the same trap. It is quite impossible to settle what was not even intended by the author to be settled. The identity of the actual author might remain a mystery. He is totally anonymous. It might be different with the pseudonymity of the corpus. The literary application of assigning these works to Dionysius the Areopagite is not part of the problem, it is part of the solution, if it is viewed as a literary methodological approach rather than an actual designator of authorship. The acceptance of this hypothesis allows the opportunity for a more constructive study of the corpus.

My hope is that it was sufficiently demonstrated that any reading of the *Areopagitica* in search of evidence of recreation of the first-century environment leads to disappointing results. Meager, historically troubling, and unprofitable biographical references in the *CD* present a poorly managed *forgery apparatus*. The whole idea to assign this corpus to the character of the first century is no less troubling. By the fifth and sixth centuries, the time for producing biblical apocryphal literature was long gone. This is especially a bad choice in the case of Dionysius the Areopagite. Apart from his brief appearance in the Book of Acts and scant hagiographical material, nothing was known about Dionysius; certainly nothing was known about his writings. It would seem there was a better choice for these works to be presented under the name of a better-established Patristic authority, known for both his orthodoxy and writings, than the Areopagite. Why would the actual author of the corpus undertake such an enterprise if he or she intended to produce a forgery?

The affiliation of the corpus with the name of the Areopagite has a different significance than simply direct association with the first-century character. The affiliation with Dionysius the Areopagite has not historical but instead metaphorical and literary significance. The actual author of the corpus, in this case, purposefully chose the name of an authoritative figure, but one who was not known for his writings. It also explains why our mysterious author is not specifically concerned about chronological discrepancies; Clement the Philosopher in the *CD* is not necessarily Clement of Rome, as John of Scythopolis suggested, but Clement of Alexandria as the immediate context of the reference points to.[13] The literary approach to write under assumed names and to include imaginative interlocutors is well-attested in antiquity and not foreign to Patristic literature. Readers perceived these assumed names and imaginative interlocutors for what they were: assumed and imaginative—and not as historical figures. Justin's *Dialogus cum Tryphone* or Methodius's *Symposium*, as well as Iamblichus's *De Mysteriis*, are good examples. Shenute, one of the famous Coptic desert fathers, wrote several letters to possibly pseudonymous addressees.[14] The pseudonymity of the *Areopagitica* in its design presents a sense of literary drama, rather than an attempt of falsification on the part of our anonymous author to portray himself as the historical Dionysius the Areopagite. It intends to play out the essential harmony between what is divine in Hellenistic thought and in Christian theology as the hymn of glory, sort of a divine comedy.

As far as the identity of the author is concerned, the scarce historical information in the corpus serves not as evidence for a lack of imagination on the part of the actual author, but as a good indication that the author of the corpus prefers to stay not pseudonymous but *explicitly anonymous* rather than to promote the alleged historical apostolicity of this corpus. "Anonymity" and "anonymous" in Greek (ἀνωνυμία and ἀνώνυμος) and as they are used in the corpus do not refer to an unknown author or document, nor do they have the additional meanings of "featureless" or "impersonal," as in English. They simply mean "namelessness" and "unspeakable," something that should not be named, or in the case of God refer to divine ineffability.[15] The effort of the author of the *CD* to remain hidden, the one who should not be named, not only seems to succeed but also goes hand in hand with Dionysian apophatic emphasis. It can be suitably explained in terms of the apophatic anthropology proposed by Stang, only not in application to pseudonymity, but to the incognito status of the author. Balthasar, as has already been noted, believes in the essentially Christian integrity of the corpus, which he sees as proven by its acceptance in the subsequent Christian tradition. This is for him a testimony to the true intent of the actual author to purposefully stay behind the scene: "Could he ever have said more than his work?"[16] Modesty, indeed, can be one of the good reasons why someone might choose to stay incognito under the cover of an assumed name. The explicit incognito status of the author only accentuates the content of the message. The Dionysian question proved to be a fruitless chase after the ghost of the author because the author of the *CD* did not want to be recognized, and he appears to do a good job in evading the watchful eyes of scholars who in vain attempted to establish his identity.

We might grant him his wish. Let him remain hidden while we can fully appreciate what he wanted to communicate. Instead of looking for the phantom of the author let us rather concentrate on the contents of his message.

Fruitless searches for the identity of the author serve only to segment and polarize the general perception of the *CD*. This corpus was seen either as Christian or Neoplatonic, either coming from Syria or from Athens or Alexandria. The author was identified as either a monk or a philosopher, Chalcedonian or Monophysite or even Nestorian,[17] Apollianrian or Origenist, compiler and forger or true genius. This deconstructive fragmentation with constructive intents, even though it provides important insights, emphasizes some particulars of the *Areopagitica* over its universals. It does not help to elucidate the message; it helps most of all to maintain certain degrees of ongoing confusion.[18] As Gersh correctly observes, "There is obviously some difference between authors who conceal doctrine and doctrines whose authors are unknown."[19] At the same time, the affiliation of these works with the name of Dionysius the Areopagite serves as an effective advertisement tool: it easily acquires the attention of potential readers.

Even though there was quite some space spent to state my hypothesis, what is proposed here points to the obvious. Any basic reading of the *Areopagitica* with the intent to search for evidence of the author's identity or intentional projection of the first-century environment would not bear any conclusive results. The author remains anonymous, while his message (that is not without obscurities of style) and his sources on the other hand are more revealing. The *CD* is the work of a Neoplatonic, more philosophically than monastically minded, Christian individual, who sees both traditions testifying to the same ultimate source of truth that comes from God. His work might be a testimony to an attempt to reconcile Hellenistic culture with emerging civilized Christian identity. He could be a monk interested in Neoplatonism, or ascetic Christian individual coming from Syria. He could live or study in Athens, or Alexandria, or Constantinople, or in different places in different stages of his life. If the attribution to the historical Dionysius the Areopagite paved the way for survival of this corpus, the attraction to its content paved the way to its real influence.

Some of the supporters or critics of the *CD* might not be fully comfortable with this approach. However, the explicit and unmasked use of Neoplatonic and Christian ideas in the corpus serves as evidence that the actual author was a Neoplatonic Christian who seriously contemplated that such agreement is possible: the harmonious hymn to God that is inspired by God, came from God, and now returns to God. Modern Dionysian scholarship amply analyzed and scrutinized many important aspects that come from late Neoplatonism and Patristic tradition to demonstrate that our author is well versed in these areas. Often the scholarship was done from a disjointed, one-sided perspective, where more emphasis was put on either Neoplatonic or Christian ideas. Considering the Christian and Neoplatonic content of the *CD* from a balanced perspective, not just acknowledging that they are present and then trying to emphasize one side of them, might help to appreciate, if not necessarily agree with, the masterful genius of the mysterious author and what he wanted to accomplish, as well as to explain why he chose the names for his heroes that he did. Perhaps, keeping himself in mind he stated, "The man in union with truth knows clearly that all is well with him, even if everyone else thinks that he has gone out of his mind. What they fail to see, naturally, is that he has gone out of the path of error and has in his real faith arrived at truth."[20]

Notes

1 Ivánka, "La Signification historique du 'Corpus Areopagiticum'," 5–24; idem, *Plato Christianus*.
2 Hathaway, *Hierarchy and the Definition of Order*, 17–19, 25–29. See ch. 2, endnote 69, p. 45.
3 Balthasar, "Denys," 2:149.
4 Schäfer, *Philosophy of Dionysius the Areopagite*.
5 Perl, *Theophany*.
6 Wear and Dillon, *Dionysius the Areopagite and the Neoplatonist Tradition*.
7 See *Prol*. PG 4:20D—21A, cf. Suchla, ed., *Corpus Dionysiacum IV/1*, 108–9.
8 Rorem and Lamoreaux, *John of Scythopolis and the Dionysian Corpus*, 51–52.
9 Rosemary Arthur, "A Sixth-Century Origenist: Stephen bar Sudhaili and His Relationship With Ps-Dionysius," *Studia Patristica* 35 (2001): 369–73; idem, *Pseudo-Dionysius as Polemicist*, 15–19.
10 Arthur, *Pseudo-Dionysius as Polemicist*, 59–61.
11 Arthur, *Pseudo-Dionysius as Polemicist*, 16.
12 Louth, *Denys the Areopagite*, 10.
13 Rorem and Lamoreaux, *John of Scythopolis and the Dionysian Corpus*, 101. Cf. *DN* 5.9 (824D-825A); and Clement of Alexandria, *Strom*. 8.29.1–2.
14 Frank R. Trombley, *Hellenic Religion and Christianization c. 370–529* (Leiden: Brill, 2001), 2:214.
15 *DN* 1.1 (588B); 1.6 (596A, three times); 1.7 (596C); and 7.1 (865C).
16 Balthasar, "Denys," 2:149.
17 If arguments for Monophysite or Neochalcedonian sympathies in the *CD* are among the most commonly discussed in antiquity and modern scholarship, extreme dyophysite (Nestorian) Christology is more debatable; nevertheless, it is also a part of scholarly discourse. See revived by István Perczel Evans's hypothesis, Perczel, "Once Again on Dionysius the Areopagite and Leontius of Byzantium," in *Die Dionysius-Rezeption im Mittelalter*, eds. Tzotcho Boiadjiev, Georgi Kapriev, and Andreas Speer (Turnhout, Belgium: Brepols Publishers, 2000), 41–85; cf. David Evans, "Leontius of Byzantium and Dionysius the Areopagite," *Études Byzantines* 7 (1980): 1–34.
18 Cf. Schäfer, *Philosophy of Dionysius the Areopagite*, 19–21.
19 Gersh, "The Pseudonymity of Dionysius the Areopagite and the Platonic Tradition," 130.
20 *DN* 7.4 (872D); Pseudo-Dionysius, *The Complete Works*, 110.

Selected bibliography

Dionysian texts

Pseudo-Dionysius. *Corpus Dionysiacum I: De Divinis Nominibus*. Edited by Beate Regina Suchla. Patristische Texte und Studien 33. Berlin: Walter de Gruyter, 1990.
———. *Corpus Dionysiacum II: De Coelesti Hierarchia, De Ecclesiastica Hierarchia, De Mystica Theologia, Epistulae*. Edited by Günter Hail and Adolf Martin Ritter. Patristische Texte und Studien 36. Berlin: Walter de Gruyter, 1991.

English translations

Pseudo-Dionysius. *Dionysius the Areopagite: On the Divine Names and Mystical Theology*. Translated by C. E. Rolt. London: S.P.C.K., 1972.
———. *The Complete Works*. Translated by Colm Luibheid and Paul Rorem. The Classics of Western Spirituality. New York, NY: Paulist Press, 1987.
———. *The Ecclesiastical Hierarchy*. Translated and annotated by Thomas L. Campbell. Washington, DC: University Press of America, 1981.
———. "The Letters." In *Hierarchy and the Definition of Order in the Letters of Pseudo-Dionysius: A Study in the Form and Meaning of the Pseudo-Dionysian Writings*. Edited by Ronald F. Hathaway, 129–60. The Hague: Nijhoff, 1969.
———. *The Works of Dionysius the Areopagite*. Translated by John Parker. Merrick, NY: Richwood Publishing Co., 1976.
Pseudo-Dionysius Areopagita. *The Mystical Theology and the Celestial Hierarchies of Dionysius the Areopagite*. Fintry, UK: Shrine of Wisdom, 1949.
Pseudo-Dionysius Areopagita. *The Divine Names and Mystical Theology*. Translated by John D. Jones. Mediaeval Philosophical Texts in Translation 21. Milwaukee, WI: Marquette University Press, 1980.

Cited and referenced sources

Armstrong, A. Hilary. "Plotinus and Christianity." In *Platonism in Late Antiquity*. Edited by Stephen Gersh and Charles Kannengiesser, 115–30. Notre Dame, IN: University of Notre Dame Press, 1992.

Selected bibliography

Arthur, Rosemary A. "A Sixth-Century Origenist: Stephen Bar Sudhaili and His Relationship With Ps-Dionysius." *Studia Patristica* 35 (2001): 369–73.

———. *Pseudo-Dionysius as Polemicist: The Development and Purpose of the Angelic Hierarchy in Sixth Century Syria*. Burlington, VT: Ashgate, 2008.

Athanassiadi, Polymnia. "Persecution and Response in Late Paganism: The Evidence of Damascius." *The Journal of Hellenic Studies* 113 (1993): 1–29.

Balthasar, Hans Urs von. "Das Scholienwerk des Johannes von Scythopolis." *Scholastik* 15 (1940): 16–38. English translation, "The Problem of the Scholia to Pseudo-Dionysius." In *Cosmic Liturgy: The Universe According to Maximus the Confessor*. Translated by Brian Daley, 357–87. San Francisco, CA: Ignatius Press, 2003.

———. "Denys." In *The Glory of the Lord: A Theological Aesthetics*. Translated by Andrew Louth, Francis McDonagh, and Brian McNeil, 2:144–210. New York, NY: Crossroad Publishing, 1984.

Beeley, Christopher A. *The Unity of Christ: Continuity and Conflict in Patristic Tradition*. New Haven, CT: Yale University Press, 2012.

Berardino, Angelo Di, editor. *Patrology: The Eastern Fathers from the Council of Chalcedon (451) to John of Damascus (†750)*. Cambridge, UK: James Clarke & Co, 2006.

Berardino, Angelo Di, and Basil Studer, editors. *The Patristic Period: Vol. 1 of History of Theology*. Collegeville, MN: The Liturgical Press, 1997.

Brons, Bernhard. "Sekundäre Textparteien im Corpus Pseudo-Dionysiacum? Literarkritische Beobachtungen zu ausgewählten Textstellen." *Nachrichten der Akademie der Wissenschaften in Göttingen: Philologisch-Historische Klasse* 5 (1975): 99–140.

Bulhak, Emmanuel. *Authenticité des oeuvres de saint Denys l'Aréopagite, évêque d'Athènes et de Lutetia in Parisiis et sa réintégration sur la siège épiscopal de Paris*. Rome, 1938.

Coakley, Sarah, and Charles M. Stang, editors. *Re-Thinking Dionysius the Areopagite*. Oxford: Wiley-Blackwell, 2009.

Copp, John Dixon. *Dionysius the Pseudo-Areopagite: Man of Darkness: Man of Light*. Lewiston, NY: Edwin Mellen Press, 2007.

Damascius. *Problems and Solutions Concerning First Principles*. Translated with Introduction and Notes by Sara Ahbel-Rappe. Oxford: Oxford University Press, 2010.

———. *The Philosophical History*. Translated by Polymnia Athanassiadi. Athens, Greece: Apamea, 1999.

Delaporte, Marianne M. "He Darkens Me With Brightness: The Theology of Pseudo-Dionysius in Hilduin's Vita of Saint Denis." *Religion & Theology* 13 (2006): 219–46.

Engelhardt, Johann G. *Dissertatio de Dionysio Areopagita plotinizante praemissis observationibus de historia theologiae mysticae rite tractanda: Sectio secunda quam auctoritate reverendissimi theologorum ordinis in Academia Friderico-Alexandrina die 28 Nov. MDCCCXX. horis pomeridianis respondente pro facultate docendi publico iudicio submittet*. Erlangae: Typis Hilpertianis, 1820.

Esbroeck, Michel van. "Peter the Iberian and Dionysius Areopagita: Honigmann's Thesis Revisited." *Orientalia Christiana Periodica* 59 (1993): 217–27.

Evans, David. "Leontius of Byzantium and Dionysius the Areopagite." *Études Byzantines* 7 (1980): 1–34.

Fedotov, George P. *The Russian Religious Mind: Kievan Christianity: The 10th to the 13th Centuries.* New York, NY: Harper Torchbooks, 1960.

Frede, Michael. "Monotheism and Pagan Philosophy in Later Antiquity." In *Pagan Monotheism in Late Antiquity.* Edited by Polymnia Athanassiadi and Michael Frede, 41–67. Oxford: Clarendon Press, 1999.

Gavrilyuk, Paul. "Did Pseudo-Dionysius Live in Constantinople?" *Vigiliae Christianae* 62 (2008): 505–14.

Gersh, Stephen. *From Iamblichus to Eriugena: An Investigation of the Prehistory and Evolution of the Pseudo-Dionysian Tradition.* Studienz zur Problemgeschichte der Antiken und Mittelalterlichen Philosophie 8. Leiden: Brill, 1978.

———. "The Pseudonymity of Dionysius the Areopagite and the Platonic Tradition." In *Neoplatonismo Pagano vs Neoplatonismo Christiano: Identità e Intersezioni.* Edited by Maria di Pasquale and Concetto Martello, 99–130. Catania, Spain: Cooperative Universitaria Editrece Catanese di Magistero, 2006.

Golitzin, Alexander. "Dionysius Areopagita: A Christian Mysticism?" *Pro Ecclesia* 12 (2003): 161–212.

———. *Et Introibo Ad Altare Dei: The Mystagogy of Dionysius Areopagita: With Special Reference to Its Predecessors in the Eastern Christian Tradition.* Analekta Blatadõn 59. Thessaloniki: Patriarchikon Idruma Paterikõn Meletõn, 1994.

———. *Mystagogy: A Monastic Reading of Dionysius Areopagita.* Edited by Bogdan G. Bucur. Collegeville, MN: Liturgical Press, 2013.

———. "The Mysticism of Dionysius Areopagita: Platonist or Christian?" *Mystics Quarterly* 19 (1993): 98–114.

Griffith, Rosemary. "Neo-Platonism and Christianity: Pseudo-Dionysius and Damascius." *Studia Patristica* 29 (1997): 238–43.

Grumel, Venance. "Autour de la question pseudo-Dionysienne." *Revue des études Byzantines* 13 (1955): 21–49.

Harnack, Adolf. *History of Dogma.* Eugene, OR: Wipf and Stock, 1997.

Hathaway, Ronald F. *Hierarchy and the Definition of Order in the Letters of Pseudo-Dionysius: A Study in the Form and Meaning of the Pseudo-Dionysian Writings.* The Hague: Nijhoff, 1969.

Hausherr, Irénée. "Doutes au sujet du 'Divin Denys." *Orientalia Christiana Periodica* 2 (1936): 484–90.

Honigmann, Ernst. *Pierre l'Ibérien et les écrits du pseudo Denys l'Aréopagite.* Brussels: Académie Royale de Belgique, 1952.

Iamblichus. *De Mysteriis.* Translated by Emma C. Clarke, John M. Dillon, and Jackson P. Hershbell. Atlanta, GA: Society of Biblical Literature, 2003.

Ivánka, Endre von. "La Signification historique du 'Corpus Areopagiticum'." *Recherches de Science Religieuse* 36 (1949): 5–24.

———. *Plato Christianus: Übernahme und Umgestaltung des Platonismus durch die Väter.* Einsiedeln: Johannes Verlag, 1964.

Selected bibliography

Jahn, Albert. *Eclogae e Proclo de Philosophia Chaldaica; sive de doctrina oraculorum Chaldaicorum.* Halle: Pfeffer, 1891.

John of Scythopolis. *Corpus Dionysiacum IV/1: Ioannis Scythopolitani Prologus et Scholia in Dionysii Areopagitae Librum De Divinis Nominibus cum Additamentis Interpretum Aliorum.* Edited by Beate Regina Suchla. Patristische Texte und Studien 62. Berlin: Walter de Gruyter, 2011.

Kenney, John Peter. "Monotheism and Polytheistic Elements in Classical Mediterranean Spirituality." In *Classical Mediterranean Spirituality.* Edited by A. H. Armstrong, 269–92. New York, NY: Crossroad Publishing, 1986.

Kharlamov, Vladimir. *The Beauty of the Unity and the Harmony of the Whole: The Concept of Theosis in the Theology of Pseudo-Dionysius the Areopagite.* Eugene, OR: Wipf and Stock, 2009.

Koch, Hugo. "Proklus als Quelle des Pseudo-Dionysius Areopagita in der Lehre vom Bösen." *Philologus* 54 (1895): 438–54.

———. *Pseudo-Dionysius Areopagita in Seinen Beziehungen zum Neuplatonismus und Mysterienwesen.* Mainz: Verlag von Franz Kirchleim, 1900.

Kojève, Alexandre. *Essai d'une histoire raisonnée de la philosophie païenne III.* Paris: Gallimard, 1973.

Lankila, Tuomo. "The *Corpus Areopagiticum* as a Crypto-Pagan Project." *Journal for Late Antique Religion and Culture* 5 (2011): 14–40.

Lequien, Michaelis. "De quibusdam auctoritatibus, quibus Eutychesaliique unius in Christo nature assertores haeresim suam tuebantur." In PG 94:261–314.

Lilla, Salvatore. "Introduzione allo studio dello Ps. Dionigi l'Areopagita." *Augustianum* 22 (1982): 568–71.

Louth, Andrew. *Denys the Areopagite*, Outstanding Christian Thinkers. London: G. Chapman, 1989.

———. *The Origins of the Christian Mystical Tradition from Plato to Denys.* Oxford: Clarendon Press, 1981.

———. "The Reception of Dionysius up to Maximus the Confessor." In *Re-Thinking Dionysius the Areopagite.* Edited by Sarah Coakley and Charles M. Stang, 43–53. Oxford: Wiley-Blackwell, 2009.

Mali, Franz. "Hat die Schrift 'De symbolica theologia' von Dionysius Ps.-Areopagita gegeben? Anmerkungen zu den Nachrichten des Sergius von Rēš'ainā über Dionysius Ps.-Areopagita." In *Syriaca. Zur Geschichte, Theologie, Liturgie und Gegenwartslage der syrischen Kirche 2: Deutsches Syrologen-Symposium (Juli 2000, Wittenberg).* Edited by Martin Tamcke, 213–24. Hamburg: Lit, 2002.

Mango, Cyril. *Byzantium: The Empire of the New Rome.* London: Phoenix, 2005.

Mazzucchi, Carlo Maria. "Damascio, autore del 'Corpus Dionysiacum', e il dialogo Περὶ πολιτικῆς ἐπιστήμης." *Aevum* 80 (2006): 299–334.

McGinn, Bernard. *The Foundations of Mysticism: Origins to the Fifth Century.* New York, NY: Crossroad Publishing, 1995.

———. *The Growth of Mysticism: Gregory the Great Through the 12th Century.* New York, NY: Crossroad Publishing, 1994.

———. *The Mystical Thought of Meister Eckhart: The Man from Whom God Hid Nothing.* New York, NY: Crossroad Publishing, 2001.

———. "The Negative Element in the Anthropology of John the Scot." In *Jean Scot Érigène et l'histoire de la philosophie: Actes du II Colloque international Jean Scot Erigène*. Edited by René Roques, 315–25. Paris: Éditions du Centre national de la recherche scientifique, 1977.
Meredith, Anthony. "Asceticism: Christian and Greek." *The Journal of Theological Studies* 27 (October 1976): 313–32.
Merkur, Daniel. "Reflections on the Meaning of Theosophy." *Theosophical History* 7 (1998): 18–34.
Müller, Hermann Friedrich. *Dionysios, Proklos, Plotinos: Ein historischer Beitrag zur neuplatonischen Philosophie*. Münster: Aschendorff, 1926.
Nasta, Mihai. "Quatre Etats de la Textualité dans l'Histoire du Corpus Dionyseinne." In *Denys l'Aréopagite et sa Posterité en Orient et en Occident*. Edited by Ysabel de Andia, 31–65. Paris: Institut d'Études Augustiniennes, 1997.
Perczel, István. "Denys l'Aréopagite, lecteur d'Origène." In *Origeniana Séptima: Orígenes in den Auseinandersetzungen des 4. Jahrhunderts*. Edited by Wolfgang A. Bienert and Uwe Kühneweg, 673–710. Leuven: Leuven University Press and Uitgeverij Peeters, 1999.
———."Once Again on Dionysius the Areopagite and Leontius of Byzantium." In *Die Dionysius-Rezeption im Mittelalter*. Edited by Tzotcho Boiadjiev, Georgi Kapriev, and Andreas Speer, 41–85. Turnhout, Belgium: Brepols Publishers, 2000.
———. "Ps. Dionysius and Palestinian Origenism." In *The Sabaite Heritage in the Orthodox Church*. Edited by Joseph Patrich, 261–82. Louvain: Peeters Publishers, 2001.
———. "The Earliest Syriac Reception of Dionysius." In *Re-Thinking Dionysius the Areopagite*. Edited by Sarah Coakley and Charles M. Stang, 27–41. Oxford: Wiley-Blackwell, 2009.
———. "The Pseudo-Didymian 'De trinitate' and Pseudo-Dionysius the Areopagite: A Preliminary Study." *Studia Patristica* 58 (2013): 83–108.
Perl, Eric David. *Theophany: The Neoplatonic Philosophy of Dionysius the Areopagite*. Albany, NY: State University of New York Press, 2007.
Places, Édouard des, Irénée H. Dalmais, and Gustave Bardy, editors. "Denys l'Aréopagite (Le Pseudo-)." In *Dictionnaire de spiritualité ascétique et mystique*, 3:244–429. Paris: Beauchesne, 1957.
Proclus. *Hymnes et prières*. Translated by Henri-Dominique Saffrey. Paris: Arfuyen, 1994.
———. *Procli Commentarium in Platonis Parmenidem*. Edited by Victor Cousin. Hildesheim, Germany: Georg Olms Verlag, 1961.
———. *Proclus' Commentary on Plato's Parmenides*. Translated by Glenn R. Morrow and John M. Dillon. Princeton, NJ: Princeton University Press, 1987.
Putnam, Caroline Canfield. *Beauty in the Pseudo-Denis*. Washington, DC: Catholic University of America Press, 1960.
Ramelli, Ilaria. *The Christian Doctrine of Apokatastasis: A Critical Assessment from the New Testament to Eriugena*. Leiden: Brill, 2013.
Riedinger, Utto. "Pseudo-Dionysios Areopagites, Pseudo-Kaisarios und die Akoimeten." *Byzantinische Zeitschrift* 52 (1956): 276–96.

Riordan, William. *Divine Light: The Theology of Denys the Areopagite*. San Francisco, CA: Ignatius Press, 2008.
Roques, René. *L'univers dionysien: Structure hiérarchique du monde selon le Pseudo-Denys*. Paris: Aubier, 1954.
Rorem, Paul. *Biblical and Liturgical Symbols within the Pseudo-Dionysian Synthesis*. Studies and Texts (Pontifical Institute of Mediaeval Studies) 71. Toronto: Pontifical Institute of Mediaeval Studies, 1984.
———. *Pseudo-Dionysius: A Commentary on the Texts and an Introduction to Their Influence*. Oxford: Oxford University Press, 1993.
———. "The Uplifting Spirituality of Pseudo-Dionysius." In *Christian Spirituality: Origins to the Twelfth Century*. Edited by Bernard McGinn, John Meyendorff, and Jean Leclercq, 132–51. New York, NY: Crossroad Publishing, 1985.
Rorem, Paul, and John C. Lamoreaux. *John of Scythopolis and the Dionysian Corpus: Annotating the Areopagite*. Oxford Early Christian Studies. Oxford: Clarendon Press, 1998.
———. "John of Scythopolis on Apollinarian Christology and the Pseudo-Areopagite's True Identity." *Church History* 62 (1993): 469–82.
Rutledge, Denys. *Cosmic Theology: The Ecclesiastical Hierarchy of Pseudo-Denys: An Introduction*. London: Routledge and Kegan Paul, 1964.
Saffrey, Henri-Dominique. "New Objective Links Between the Pseudo-Dionysius and Proclus." In *Neoplatonism and Christian Thought*. Edited by Dominic O'Meara, 64–74. Albany, NY: State University of New York Press, 1982.
———. "Un lien objectif entre le Pseudo-Denys et Proclus." *Studia Patristica* 9 (1966): 98–105.
Schäfer, Christian. *Philosophy of Dionysius the Areopagite: An Introduction to the Structure and the Content of the Treatise on the Divine Names*. Boston, MA: Brill, 2006.
Sergius of Reshaina, and Sherwood, Polycarp. "Mimro de Serge de Resayna sur la vie spirituelle." *L'Orient Syrien* 5 (1960): 433–57; 6 (1961): 96–115, 122–56.
Sheldon-Williams, I. P. "The ps. Dionysius and the Holy Hierotheus." *Studia Patristica* 8.2 (1966): 108–17.
Sicherl, Martin. "Ein neuplatonischer Hymnus unter den Gedichten Gregors von Nazianz." In *Gonimos: Neoplatonic and Byzantine Studies Presented to Leendert G. Westerink at 75*. Edited by J. Duffy and J. Peradotto, 61–83. Buffalo, NJ: Arethusa, 1988.
Sint, Josef A. *Pseudonymität im Altertum, ihre Formen und ihre Gründe*. Innsbruck: Wagner, 1960.
Speyer, Wolfgang. *Die literarsche Fälschung im beidnischen und christlischen Altertum*. München: C. H. Beck, 1971.
Stang, Charles. *Apophasis and Pseudonymity in Dionysius the Areopagite: "No Longer I"*. Oxford: Oxford University Press, 2012.
———. " 'Being Neither Oneself Nor Someone Else': The Apophatic Anthropology of Dionysius the Areopagite." In *Apophatic Bodies*. Edited by Chris Boesel and Catherine Keller, 59–75. New York, NY: Fordham University Press, 2010.

———. "Dionysius, Paul and the Significance of the Pseudonym." In *Re-Thinking Dionysius the Areopagite*. Edited by Sarah Coakley and Charles M. Stang, 11–25. Oxford: Wiley-Blackwell, 2009.

Stiglmayr, Josef. "Das Aufkommen der ps.-dionysischen Schriften und ihr Eindringen in die christliche Literatur bis zum Lateranconcil 649: Ein zweiter Beitrag zur Dionysius Frage." *Jahresbericht des öffenlichen Privatgymnasiums an der Stelle matutina zu Feldkirch* 4 (1895): 3–96.

———. "Der Neuplatoniker Proclus als Vorlage des sog: Dionysius Areopagita in der Lehre vom Übel." *Historisches Jahrbuch* 16 (1895): 253–73, 721–48.

———. "Der sogenannte Dionysius Areopagita und Severus von Antiochien." *Scholastik* 3 (1928): 1–27, 161–89.

———. "Um eine Ehrenrettung des Severus von Antiochen." *Scholastik* 7 (1933): 52–67.

Suchla, Beate Regina. "Die Überlieferung des Prologs des Johannes von Skythopolis zum griechischen Corpus Dionysiacum Areopagiticum: Ein weiterer Beitrag zur Überlieferungsgeschichte des CD." *Nachrichten der Akademie der Wissenschaften in Göttingen: I. Philologisch-Historische Klasse* 4 (1984): 176–88.

———. *Dionysius Areopagita: Leben, Werk, Wirkung*. Wien: Herder, 2008.

———. "Eine Redaktion des griechischen Corpus Dionysiacum Areopagiticum im Umkreis des Johannes von Skythopolis, des Verfassers von Prolog und Scholien: Ein dritter Beitrag zur Überlieferungsgeschichte des CD." *Nachrichten der Akademie der Wissenschaften in Göttingen: I. Philologisch-Historische Klasse* 4 (1985): 177–93.

Trombley, Frank R. *Hellenic Religion and Christianization c. 370–529*. Leiden: Brill, 2001.

Turner, Denys. *The Darkness of God: Negativity in Christian Mysticism*. Cambridge: Cambridge University Press, 1995.

Vogel, Cornelia J. de. "Platonism and Christianity: A Mere Antagonism or a Profound Common Ground?" *Vigiliae Christianae* 39 (1985): 1–62.

Wallis, Richard T. *Neoplatonism*, 2nd ed. Indianapolis, IN: Hackett Publishing Company, 1995.

Wear, Sarah Klitenic, and John Dillon. *Dionysius the Areopagite and the Neoplatonic Tradition*. Hampshire, UK: Ashgate, 2007.

Wesche, Kenneth Paul. "Christological Doctrine and Liturgical Interpretation in Pseudo-Dionysius." *St. Vladimir's Theological Quarterly* 33 (1989): 53–73.

Westcott, Brooke. "Dionysius the Areopagite." *Contemporary Review* 5 (1867): 1–27.

Wilmart, André, and Eugène Tisserant. "Fragments grecs et latins de l'Évangile de Barthélemy." *Revue biblique* 10 (1913): 161–90.

INDEX

Aeneas 68–9
Ahbel-Rappe, Sara 44
Alexandria, Alexandrian 4, 28, 30, 68, 83
Ammonius 69
Andia, Ysabel de 42
Apollinarianism 74, 80, 83
Apostolic Fathers 54, 55, 57, 61, 62
Aristotle 75, 77
Armstrong, A. Hilary 70, 76, 77, 85
Arthur, Rosemary 2, 7, 13, 18, 21–2, 29, 31, 41, 43, 44, 50–1, 52, 58, 65, 66, 67, 80, 84
asceticism 4, 13, 25, 28–9, 62, 69–70, 83
Athanasius of Alexandria 47
Athanassiadi, Polymnia 30–1, 44, 76
Athens/Athenian 4, 5, 6, 14, 15, 20, 24, 30–1, 33, 55, 57, 63, 65, 73, 78, 83
Augustine of Hippo 24, 49

Balthasar, Hans Urs von 5, 8, 10–11, 12, 15, 17, 18, 19, 22, 42–3, 50, 52, 58, 66, 78, 79, 82, 84
Bardy, Gustave 42
Bartholomew, the apostle 54, 55, 57, 64
Basil of Caesarea 30, 47
Beeley, Christopher 47, 52
Berardino, Angelo Di 44
Brons, Bernard 42, 52, 67
Bulhak, Emmanuel 41

Campbell, Thomas 31, 39, 44, 46, 66, 74, 77
Chalcedon/Chalcedonian 34, 35, 36, 61, 81, 83, 84
Christology in the *CD* 35–6, 63

chronological discrepancies 3, 60–1, 73, 82
Clement of Alexandria 57, 60, 65, 82
Clement of Rome 54, 63, 82
Clement the Philosopher 54, 57, 82
Constantine, the emperor 68
Copp, John 3, 8, 41–2, 53, 66
Cyril of Alexandria 48

Dalmais, Irénée 42
Damascius 30–1, 33, 34, 53, 71, 78, 79
Delaporte, Marianne 67
Didymus the Blind 23
Dillon, John 6, 8, 33, 44, 45, 51, 53, 78, 84
Dionysian society 6, 21, 54–67
Dionysius of Corinth 65
Dionysius of Paris 1, 63, 67
Domitian, the emperor 60, 61, 66
Dormition of Mary 3, 55, 58, 64–5

Eastern Orthodox Christianity 5, 11, 12, 14, 25, 26, 29, 34, 39, 40, 65, 71, 73, 81
Engelhardt, Johann 1, 6
Ephrem the Syrian 27
Erasmus 1
Esbroeck, Michel van 8, 45
Eunapius 30, 44
Eusebius of Caesarea 9, 27, 44, 65, 66
Evans, David 84

Fedotov, George 72, 77
Frede, Michael 77

Gavrilyuk, Paul 7
Gersh, Stephen 5, 8, 33, 45, 59, 66, 83, 84

Index

Golitzin, Alexander 4, 7, 8, 10, 11, 12–14, 17, 18, 25–7, 28, 29, 31, 42, 43, 44, 45, 50, 52, 75, 77, 79
Greek language 14, 20, 31–2, 40, 41
Greek philosophy 5, 13, 34, 37–8, 57, 64, 65, 68–75, 82
Gregory of Nazianzus 23, 30, 47, 76
Gregory Palamas 29
Griffith, Rosemary 45
Grumel, Venance 1, 6

Harnack, Adolf 29, 44
Hathaway, Ronald 7, 42, 43, 44, 45, 51, 71–2, 77, 78–9, 84
Hausherr, Irénée 42, 52
Hellenistic culture 5–6, 13, 14, 26, 28, 30, 32, 37, 38, 41, 57, 64, 68–75, 76, 83
Hierocles 68–9
Hierotheus 54, 57–9, 64, 65, 66, 79
Hilduin 42, 63, 67
Honigmann, Ernst 44
Hymn to God (Ὕμνος εἰς θεόν) 23
Hypatia 68

Iamblichus 5, 25, 44, 69, 82
Ignatius of Antioch 54, 60, 61
integrity of the *CD* 20, 21–4
Irenaeus 60
Ivánka, Endre von 43, 78, 84

Jahn, Albert 23, 43
James, the brother of Jesus 54, 55, 57, 58
Jerusalem 5, 55, 73
John, the apostle 11–12, 14, 54, 55, 57, 60
John Chrysostom 30
John of Scythopolis 3, 9, 26, 40, 50, 51, 54, 56, 60, 61, 65, 66, 67, 79, 82
John Philoponus 3–4, 9, 28, 50, 51, 65, 69
John Scottus Eriugena 15, 63
Justin 38, 82
Justin, the emperor 71
Justinian, the emperor 31, 71

Kenney, John 77
Kharlamov, Vladimir 9, 52
Koch, Hugo 1, 2, 6, 21, 41, 74
Kojève, Alexandre 45

Lamoreaux, John 1, 7, 8, 9, 56, 65, 66, 79, 84
Lankila, Tuomo 7, 45
Leontius of Byzantium 27
Leontius of Jerusalem 27
Lequien, Michaelis 7
Libanius 30
Lilla, Salvatore 7
Lorenzo Valla 1
Louth, Andrew 9, 22, 26–7, 28, 35, 42, 43, 44, 45, 64, 66, 67, 77, 81, 84

Mali, Franz 42
Mango, Cyril 77
Martin Luther 1
Maximus the Confessor 27
Mazzucchi, Carlo Maria 45
McGinn, Bernard 15, 19, 24, 43
Meister Eckhart 15
Merkur, Daniel 44
Messalianism 13
Methodius of Olympus 82
monasticism/monastic 4, 10, 12–14, 24, 25–30, 62, 69, 79, 83
Monophysitism 1, 2, 13–14, 24, 29, 31, 34, 35, 36, 74, 80, 83, 84
Moses 5, 15, 38
Mother of God 3, 49, 55, 57, 59, 64–5

Nasta, Mihai 42, 67
Neoplatonism 1, 3, 4, 6, 10, 13, 14, 15, 18, 20–1, 24, 25, 26, 27, 28–30, 31, 32–3, 34, 37, 38, 40, 41, 51, 52, 53, 59, 64, 65, 68–75, 77, 78, 79, 80, 83–4
Nestorianism 36, 83, 84
Numenius 9

Origen 24, 30, 47, 58
Origenist controversy 25, 34, 35, 50, 58, 73, 74, 80, 83

Patristic apologetics 5, 38, 78, 79
Patristic tradition 4, 11, 14, 26, 29, 31, 33–9, 40, 41, 47–8, 51–2, 57, 60, 68, 70, 75, 82, 83–4
Paul, the apostle 5, 14, 26, 51, 54, 55–7, 58, 59, 60, 63, 65, 76, 79
Pelikan, Jaroslav 39

94 *Index*

Perczel, István 2, 7, 22–3, 42, 43, 50, 52, 58, 61, 66, 67, 84
Perl, Eric 32–3, 45, 78, 84
Peter, the apostle 54, 55, 58
Peter Abelard 1
Peter the Fuller 2
Peter the Iberian 7, 8, 14, 31, 44–5
Places, Édouard des 42
Plato 5, 38, 58, 59, 62, 63, 64, 67, 71, 75
Platonism 32, 68, 70
Plotinus 32, 53, 69
Polycarp of Smyrna 54, 60, 61, 66
Porphyry 5
Proclus 1, 4, 5, 23, 25, 29, 31, 32, 34, 37, 50, 51, 53, 58, 59, 69, 71, 77, 80
Protestant Christianity 1, 34
Putnam, Caroline 4, 7, 8

Rahner, Karl 55
Ramelli, Ilaria 4, 8, 58, 66
Rayez, André 46
Riedinger, Utto 7
Riordan, William 10, 11–12, 15, 17, 18
Roman-Byzantine Christian identity 5–6, 32, 41, 64, 72–3, 76, 77, 83
Roman Catholic Christianity 5, 34
Roques, René 22, 42, 43
Rorem, Paul 1, 4, 7, 8, 9, 14, 18, 42, 46, 56, 60, 65, 66, 67, 79, 84
Rutledge, Denys 73, 77

Saffrey, Henri-Dominique 7, 23, 43, 50, 52
Schäfer, Christian 10, 16–17, 19, 37, 42, 45, 66, 77, 78, 84
Sergius of Reshaina 22–3, 28, 50, 51, 53
Severus of Antioch 1–2, 24, 50, 51
Shenute 82
Sherwood, Polycarp 53

Sicherl, Martin 23, 43
Sint, Josef A. 8
Socrates 58, 71
Sosipater 37, 54
soteriology 36, 69
Speyer, Wolfgang 8
Stang, Charles 10, 14–16, 17, 18, 19, 23, 42, 66, 79, 82
Stephen Bar Sudhaili 80
Stiglmayr, Josef 1, 2, 6, 7, 21, 24, 41, 74
Suchla, Beate 2, 3, 7, 8, 46
Synesius of Cyrene 68
Syrian background of the *CD* 2, 6, 7, 10, 12–14, 15, 17, 20, 22, 24–7, 28–9, 79, 80, 83
Syrianus 59

Thearchy 35, 36, 45
Theodosius I, the emperor 68
theurgy 36, 58, 69
Timothy 27, 54, 55–6, 57, 60, 64, 66
Tisserant, Eugène 64
Titus 54
Trombley, Frank 84
Turner, Denys 15, 19

Vogel, Cornelia J. de 45, 77

Wallis, Richard 30, 44, 76
Wear, Sarah 6, 8, 33, 44, 45, 51, 53, 78, 84
Wesche, Kenneth Paul 77
Westcott, Brooke 74, 77
William Grocyn 1
Wilmart, André 64

Zacharias Scholasticus 69
Zeno, the emperor 71

For Product Safety Concerns and Information please contact our EU
representative GPSR@taylorandfrancis.com
Taylor & Francis Verlag GmbH, Kaufingerstraße 24, 80331 München, Germany

www.ingramcontent.com/pod-product-compliance
Lightning Source LLC
Chambersburg PA
CBHW070741230426
43669CB00014B/2532